TUNISIA
TRAVEL GUIDE 2025

By

Cathy Dawson

COPYRIGHT

All rights reserved. No part of this publication may be reproduced, distributed, or transmitted in any form or by any means, including photocopying, recording or other electronic or mechanical methods, without the prior written permission of the publisher, except in the case of brief quotation embodied in critical reviews and certain other noncommercial uses permitted by copyright law.

Copyright by Cathy Dawson 2025

CONTENTS

INTRODUCTION 5
- WELCOME TO TUNISIA: AN OVERVIEW 5
- WHY CHOOSE TUNISIA FOR YOUR NEXT TRAVEL 8
- THE PEOPLE, CULTURE, AND TRADITIONS OF TUNISIA 14
- MY PERSONAL JOURNEY ACROSS TUNISIA 19

CHAPTER 1: TRIP PLANNING 24
- WHEN TO VISIT TUNISIA 24
- VISA AND ENTRY INFORMATIONS 29
- MONEY MATTERS: CURRENCY, EXCHANGE AND MORE 33
- HEALTH AND SAFETY TIPS 38
- PACKING GUIDE 43
- GETTING TO TUNISIA 48

CHAPTER 2: MUST-VISIT DESTINATIONS 54
- TUNIS & THE MEDINA 54
- CARTHAGE 59
- BLUE & WHITE VILLAGE OF SIDI BOU SAID 64
- EXPLORING SAHARA DESERT 69
- COASTAL GEMS: HAMMAMET, MONASTIR & DJERBA ISLAND 74
- ROMAN RUINS OF DOUGGA & EL DJEM 79
- ATLAS MOUNTAINS & KAIROUAN 84
- TOZEUR & THE CHOTT EL JERID SALT FLATS 89

CHAPTER 3: CUISINE AND DINING 94
- MUST-TRY DISHES 94
- LOCAL MARKETS & STREET FOOD 99
- WINE AND MINT TEA 103
- DINING ETIQUETTE & WHERE TO EAT 108

CHAPTER 4: CULTURAL EXPERIENCES 113
- FESTIVALS 113
- MOSQUES, CHURCHES & SYNAGOGUES 118

    Spending Your Day in a Traditional Tunisian Home.......................... 122
    Art and Craft Scene.. 127

CHAPTER 5: ADVENTURE, NATURE, & ACTIVITIES 132

    Camel Rides, Hot Air Ballooning & Desert Camping 132
    Hiking Trails & Trekking.. 137
    Diving and Snorkeling Hotspots 142
    Sustainable Tourism & Wildlife Encounters 147

CHAPTER 6: ACCOMMODATION 153

    Hotels and Resorts... 153
    Unique & Alternative Stays 158

CHAPTER 7: PRACTICAL TIPS 163

    Getting Around Tunisia: Transport Tips.. 163
    Souvenirs & Authentic Finds to Bring Home 168

CHAPTER 8: READY-TO-USE ITINERARIES 173

    3-Day Itinerary: A Weekend in Tunisia 173
    7-Day Itinerary: A Deeper Exploration 178

CONCLUSION 184

    Maximizing Your Trip To Tunisia 184

INTRODUCTION

Welcome To Tunisia: An Overview

Tunisia, a captivating country perched on the northernmost tip of Africa, offers visitors a stunning blend of Mediterranean charm, ancient history, vibrant culture, and natural beauty. Bordered by Algeria to the west, Libya to the southeast, and the shimmering Mediterranean Sea to the north and east, Tunisia covers an area of about 164,000 square kilometers. Its strategic location at the crossroads of Africa and Europe has shaped its identity for thousands of years, making it a fascinating destination for travelers seeking both adventure and cultural enrichment.

Often overlooked in favor of its larger North African neighbors, Tunisia stands out for its rich heritage, diverse landscapes, and welcoming spirit. The capital city, Tunis, is a lively metropolis that beautifully balances old and new. Visitors can wander the narrow, winding alleys of the Medina—a UNESCO World Heritage Site—before stepping into the modern city with its bustling markets, cafes, and vibrant street life.

Tunisia's appeal lies not only in its cities but also in its breathtaking natural scenery. Along its long coastline, travelers will find pristine beaches, turquoise waters, and charming seaside towns like Hammamet, Monastir, and the enchanting island of Djerba. These coastal areas offer opportunities for relaxation, water sports, and cultural exploration, often without the heavy crowds found in more commercialized Mediterranean destinations.

Moving inland, the landscape transforms dramatically. The rolling hills of the north give way to fertile plains, olive groves, and vineyards. Tunisia is one of the world's leading producers of olive oil, and visitors often have the chance to sample fresh, locally made oils. Further south, the scenery shifts once again as the Sahara Desert spreads its golden sands across the region. The desert offers unforgettable experiences like camel treks, 4x4 desert safaris, and nights spent under a canopy of stars.

Tunisia is also a country steeped in history. It was home to the ancient city of Carthage, one of the greatest powers of the ancient Mediterranean world, rivaling Rome itself. Today, visitors can explore the archaeological remains of Carthage, marvel at the Roman amphitheater of El Djem, and wander the well-preserved ruins of Dougga. These sites provide a tangible connection to the country's complex past, which includes Phoenician, Roman, Arab, Ottoman, and French influences.

Culturally, Tunisia is a melting pot of traditions, languages, and religions. While Arabic is the official language, French is widely spoken due to Tunisia's colonial history, making communication easier for many visitors. Islam is the predominant religion, and its influence can be seen in the country's architecture, festivals, and daily life. However, Tunisia is known for its tolerant and moderate approach to religion, and it maintains a diverse cultural landscape that embraces various faiths and practices.

Tunisian cuisine is another highlight for visitors. The food reflects Mediterranean and North African flavors, with dishes characterized by fresh seafood, couscous, spices, and locally grown produce. Harissa, a fiery chili paste, is a staple condiment that adds depth to many meals. Visitors often enjoy exploring local markets, where colorful displays of fruits, vegetables, spices, and handcrafted goods bring the culture to life.

The climate in Tunisia is typically Mediterranean along the coast, with hot, dry summers and mild, wet winters. Inland and southern regions experience a more arid, desert climate. This variation allows visitors to choose their preferred environment, whether it's basking in the sun along the coast or exploring the cool mountain villages or sun-scorched desert.

Another factor that makes Tunisia attractive to travelers is its accessibility and affordability. Compared to many European destinations, Tunisia offers excellent value for money. Accommodation ranges from luxury resorts to budget-friendly guesthouses, and transportation within the country is relatively inexpensive. The country's well-developed infrastructure makes it easy to move between regions by train, bus, or car.

Safety and hospitality are also essential aspects of Tunisia's travel experience. Tunisians are generally friendly, curious, and welcoming to visitors. While it's always wise to stay informed about travel advisories, Tunisia has made significant strides in maintaining security and ensuring that tourists feel comfortable during their stay.

For those interested in arts and crafts, Tunisia's markets and artisan workshops offer a variety of handmade goods such as pottery, carpets, leather products, and intricate jewelry. These items often reflect centuries-old techniques passed down through generations, making them special souvenirs of a Tunisian adventure.

Tunisia is a land of contrasts — where the past meets the present, where Mediterranean beaches meet Saharan dunes, and where tradition meets modern life. It is a country that rewards curious travelers with rich experiences, scenic beauty, and genuine human connection. Whether you're looking to lose yourself in history, soak up the sun on a quiet beach, explore vibrant markets, or journey deep into the desert, Tunisia has something to offer every type of visitor.

Why Choose Tunisia For Your Next Travel

Tunisia is a country that offers travelers an extraordinary mix of history, culture, natural beauty, and adventure. From the ancient ruins of Carthage to the sweeping sands of the Sahara Desert, Tunisia is a land of contrasts, where past and present coexist in a harmonious blend. Whether you're a history buff, a nature enthusiast, a beach lover, or an adventurer looking for new horizons, Tunisia has something for everyone. For those wondering *why visit Tunisia*, the answer is multifaceted—there is no shortage of reasons to explore this North African gem.

One of the most compelling reasons to visit Tunisia is its rich and diverse history. Tunisia's position at the crossroads of the Mediterranean and Africa has attracted numerous civilizations over the millennia, each leaving its mark on the country. Ancient ruins, like the spectacular city of Carthage, evoke the legacy of a once-great empire that rivaled Rome. The Phoenician city, destroyed in the Punic Wars, was rebuilt by the Romans, leaving behind stunning mosaics and monumental structures that continue to captivate visitors. The Roman amphitheater at El Djem, which rivals Rome's Colosseum in size and preservation, stands as a testament to Tunisia's prominence in ancient times. For those intrigued by the classical world, Tunisia offers a tangible connection to the past, with numerous archaeological sites, including Dougga and Sbeitla, showcasing the grandeur of Roman architecture and engineering.

Beyond the ruins, Tunisia is a treasure trove of Islamic history and culture. The country's role as a center of Islamic scholarship during the medieval period left a deep imprint on its cultural landscape. Kairouan, considered one of the holiest cities in Islam, is home to the Great Mosque of Kairouan, a place of pilgrimage and learning for Muslims throughout history. Visitors can experience the serenity and beauty of Tunisia's Islamic heritage by exploring its historic mosques, medinas, and vibrant souks (markets), which provide a sensory feast of sights, sounds, and smells. The country's ability to balance its Islamic traditions with a relatively liberal and secular approach makes it an intriguing destination for anyone interested in the cultural intersections between the Arab world and the West.

In addition to its historical significance, Tunisia's natural landscapes are a major draw. The country is blessed with an incredibly diverse topography, ranging from the fertile plains and olive groves of the north to the endless dunes of the Sahara in the south. Tunisia's Mediterranean coastline, with its golden beaches and crystal-clear waters, is ideal for those looking to unwind or indulge in water sports such as windsurfing, sailing, and snorkeling. Coastal towns like Hammamet, Monastir, and Sousse boast beautiful resorts and lively markets, making them perfect for a laid-back getaway.

For more active travelers, the deserts of southern Tunisia offer endless possibilities for exploration. The Sahara, one of the world's most famous and awe-inspiring landscapes, is a must-see for adventure enthusiasts. Visitors can ride camels across the dunes, spend the night in traditional desert camps under a canopy of stars, or explore the ancient troglodyte dwellings of Matmata and Tataouine, which have become iconic due to their use in the *Star Wars* films. Tunisia's desert offers not only an otherworldly experience but also an opportunity to connect with a landscape that has shaped the culture and lifestyle of the country's southern people for centuries.

Tunisia is also home to some of the most picturesque towns in the Mediterranean. Sidi Bou Said, a hilltop village near Tunis, is a photographer's dream, with its whitewashed buildings adorned with blue doors and shutters, perched on a cliff overlooking the sea. The town's narrow streets, filled with charming cafes and artisan shops, evoke the relaxed atmosphere of the Mediterranean lifestyle. In contrast, the bustling medina of Tunis offers a completely different experience, where visitors can get lost in a maze of alleys lined with souks selling traditional textiles, spices, and jewelry. The contrast between Tunisia's ancient architecture and modern urban development provides a fascinating glimpse into the country's evolving identity.

For those interested in nature, Tunisia offers several stunning national parks and nature reserves. The Ichkeul National Park, a UNESCO World Heritage site, is a haven for birdwatchers, as it is home to thousands of migratory birds, particularly during the winter months. The park's sprawling wetlands and verdant hills provide an escape into nature that contrasts beautifully with the country's arid southern regions. Similarly, the Zembra and Zembretta Islands, located off the northern coast, offer pristine natural beauty and are perfect for nature lovers seeking peaceful retreats.

Another compelling reason to visit Tunisia is its cuisine, which is a delightful reflection of the country's cultural diversity. Tunisian food is a harmonious blend of Mediterranean, Arab, and Berber influences, with flavors that range from spicy to savory, fresh to tangy. Dishes like couscous, a staple made from semolina and served with meats, vegetables, or fish, are found throughout the country. Brik, a fried pastry filled with egg, tuna, and capers, is another delicious snack that is quintessentially

Tunisian. Tunisia is also famous for its use of spices, with harissa— a fiery chili paste—adding depth to many dishes. For seafood lovers, Tunisia's coastline offers an abundance of fresh catches, including octopus, shrimp, and sardines, often prepared in flavorful, aromatic dishes.

Beyond food, Tunisia's markets and festivals are another reason to visit. The country's lively souks, especially in Tunis, Sousse, and Kairouan, offer a glimpse into the country's traditional commerce. Here, visitors can find handwoven carpets, intricate ceramics, leather goods, jewelry, and spices. The vibrant colors and textures of the markets evoke the spirit of Tunisia, where craftsmanship and tradition thrive. Tunisia is also home to many fascinating festivals, including the Carthage Film Festival, one of the most prestigious events in the Arab world, and the International Festival of the Sahara, which celebrates the country's desert heritage through music, dance, and traditional performances.

Tunisia's warm and welcoming people are another reason why visitors find the country so appealing. Tunisians are known for their hospitality, often going out of their way to make visitors feel at home. Whether it's enjoying a cup of mint tea in a family home or getting helpful directions from a local merchant, the genuine warmth and friendliness of the Tunisian people add an invaluable layer to the travel experience. Tunisia's cultural diversity and history of coexistence between different faiths and ethnicities have fostered a spirit of tolerance, which makes it a welcoming destination for all types of travelers.

In recent years, Tunisia has emerged as a more politically stable and democratic nation, following its successful revolution in 2011. This transition to democracy has opened the door for greater tourism opportunities, with modern infrastructure, improved transportation, and an emphasis on sustainability in the tourism sector. Tunisia is now recognized for offering a unique blend of North African authenticity, Mediterranean ease, and a cosmopolitan atmosphere, making it an ideal destination for those seeking something different from the more traditional Mediterranean vacation.

There are countless reasons why Tunisia should be on your travel list. Its rich history, stunning landscapes, cultural diversity, warm hospitality, and delicious cuisine make it an incredibly rewarding destination. Whether you're interested in uncovering the secrets of ancient civilizations, experiencing the vastness of the desert, or simply enjoying a beach holiday with a cultural twist, Tunisia provides an unforgettable experience. With its fascinating mix of the old and new, the peaceful and the adventurous, Tunisia is a place where travelers can discover both timeless beauty and the energy of a modern nation on the rise.

The People, Culture, and Traditions of Tunisia

The country's strategic position at the crossroads of Europe, Africa, and the Middle East has made it a melting pot of cultures, which is evident in the unique blend of traditions, languages, and customs that define Tunisian society today. Visitors to Tunisia are not only captivated by the historical sites and landscapes but also by the warmth and generosity of its people, who offer a rare glimpse into the everyday life of a nation with a deep respect for its past while embracing modernity.

At the heart of Tunisia's cultural identity is its people, who are primarily of Arab and Berber descent, with a significant number of Tunisian Jews and other minorities contributing to the country's diverse social fabric. The Arab-Berber mix has created a society that blends Mediterranean, African, and Arab customs and influences. Historically, Tunisia has been home to a number of different ethnic groups who have lived together in relative harmony, with centuries of coexistence between the Arab, Berber, Jewish, and later, the European (particularly French and Italian) communities. While the Arab influence is the most dominant, especially with the arrival of Islam in the 7th century, many Berber traditions and customs remain important, particularly in the rural areas and in southern Tunisia.

The official language of Tunisia is Arabic, specifically Modern Standard Arabic, which is used in government, media, and formal education. However, the everyday language spoken by most Tunisians is Tunisian Arabic, also known as *Derja*. This is a local dialect that incorporates influences from Arabic, Berber, French, Italian, and even Turkish, reflecting the country's long history of foreign influence. While Tunisian Arabic might sound unfamiliar to travelers, it's not too difficult to pick up some key phrases or greetings. For instance, "As-salamu alaykum" (عليكم السلام) is a common Arabic greeting meaning "Peace be upon you," and "Shukran" (شكرا) means "Thank you." French is also widely spoken in Tunisia, particularly in urban areas and in business, as the country was a French protectorate until 1956. Many Tunisians are bilingual, speaking both Arabic and French fluently, and English is increasingly spoken in tourist areas, making it relatively easy for international visitors to communicate.

Religion plays a central role in the life of most Tunisians. Islam is the dominant religion, with the vast majority of the population being Sunni Muslims. Islam profoundly shapes the daily routines, cultural practices, and traditions of the people, from the call to prayer that resonates through the streets five times a day to the month of Ramadan, when Tunisians fast from dawn to sunset. Ramadan is a time for reflection, spiritual renewal, and community. In the evenings, families and friends gather for the iftar meal, where dates, soup, and *brik* (a fried pastry filled with egg and tuna) are commonly served. The call to prayer, which marks the times for prayer throughout the day, can be heard echoing through the towns and cities, a reminder of the country's deep Islamic traditions.

Despite the overwhelming influence of Islam, Tunisia is known for its more moderate and progressive approach to religion compared to other countries in the region. The country has a strong tradition of secularism, which is enshrined in its constitution. The secular nature of the state allows for a level of personal freedom and tolerance not always seen in other Islamic countries. Tunisia has long been at the forefront of promoting women's rights, with the 1956 Code of Personal Status granting women significant legal protections, including the right to divorce and marry without the need for male guardianship. This progressive stance on women's rights has made Tunisia one of the most liberal countries in the Arab world, where women play an active role in public life, education, and the workforce.

Tunisia's Jewish community, once thriving, has dwindled over the years, but there are still small Jewish populations, particularly in the island of Djerba, where one of the oldest synagogues in the world, El Ghriba, can be found. The Jewish presence in Tunisia dates back to the Roman era, and the community has contributed significantly to the country's cultural and economic life over the centuries. Djerba, in particular, is known for its peaceful coexistence of Muslims, Jews, and Christians, offering a rare example of interfaith harmony.

Hospitality is a core value in Tunisian culture, and visitors are often struck by the generosity and friendliness of the people. Tunisians are known for being warm and welcoming, eager to share their traditions, food, and stories with foreigners. A common expression in Tunisia is *"Ahlan wa sahlan"*, which roughly translates to "Welcome, feel at home." This is not just a polite phrase; it is an embodiment of the genuine hospitality that visitors experience in Tunisia. Whether you're invited into someone's home for a cup of mint tea, or offered directions by a local merchant, you will find that Tunisians take great pride in making visitors feel comfortable. The act of sharing food, particularly couscous or a traditional tagine, is a symbol of this hospitality, and it is not uncommon for locals to go out of their way to offer visitors a meal or refreshments.

Tunisian hospitality is also reflected in the country's traditional markets, or souks, where shoppers engage in friendly banter and bargaining. While the souks can be a lively and sometimes overwhelming experience, they offer an authentic glimpse into Tunisia's commercial traditions. In many cases, merchants will offer a cup of tea or a conversation with customers, turning shopping into an opportunity for social interaction. The souks of Tunis, Kairouan, and Sousse are particularly known for their vibrant atmosphere, where one can find everything from traditional textiles, jewelry, and pottery to spices and sweets.

Tunisian culture is steeped in a number of traditions that visitors can experience throughout the year. The country celebrates a variety of festivals that highlight its cultural diversity and history. One of the most important is the annual *Carthage Film Festival*, which attracts filmmakers and cinema enthusiasts from around the world. This festival not only showcases the best of Arab and African cinema but also serves as a platform for Tunisian artists to display their work. Other cultural festivals include the *International*

Festival of the Sahara in Tozeur, which celebrates the music, dance, and crafts of Tunisia's desert culture, and the *Festival of the Medina* in Tunis, which features traditional music and performances in the historic heart of the capital. These festivals are important occasions for Tunisians to express their cultural pride and showcase their traditions to the world.

Tunisian weddings, for instance, are grand affairs that blend traditional rituals with modern celebrations. A Tunisian wedding often spans several days, with a series of pre-wedding events, including the *Henna night*, where the bride's hands and feet are decorated with intricate henna designs. The wedding day itself is marked by lavish feasts, lively music, and dancing, with both families coming together to celebrate the union. In rural areas, these traditions are more rooted in local customs, while in urban centers, the celebrations can sometimes have a more modern flair.

One of the most interesting cultural elements in Tunisia is the *medina*—the old part of the cities—where you'll find a dense maze of narrow streets, ancient architecture, and bustling markets. These historical districts, particularly in cities like Tunis, Kairouan, and Sousse, are perfect examples of the country's rich Islamic and Arab heritage. The narrow alleys, whitewashed houses, and intricate doorways are steeped in tradition, while the sounds of artisans at work and the aromas of fresh bread and spices evoke the bustling atmosphere of old Tunisia. Exploring the medina offers visitors the chance to step back in time and experience Tunisia's vibrant, historical heart.

Tunisia's people and traditions form the backbone of the country's rich cultural identity. With its unique blend of Arab, Berber, and Mediterranean influences, Tunisia offers visitors a chance to explore a society that values history, hospitality, and cultural exchange. From the daily practices of Islam to the warmth of Tunisian hospitality, from the lively souks to the quiet dignity of its rural communities, Tunisia's traditions offer a deep and rewarding experience for anyone who takes the time to engage with them. In many ways, it is the people of Tunisia—their warmth, their stories, and their deep connection to their heritage—that make this country so special for travelers.

My Personal Journey Across Tunisia

My journey through Tunisia was one of both discovery and deep reflection, a journey that unfolded layer by layer, revealing the country's incredible beauty, fascinating history, and the unspoken warmth of its people. It was a trip that not only offered a glimpse into Tunisia's past but also provided an intimate look at how the ancient and modern intertwine in this dynamic and vibrant country.

My adventure began in Tunis, the bustling capital, where the old and the new collide in a mesmerizing mix. Walking through the streets of Tunis felt like stepping into a time machine—every corner seemed to whisper stories from the past. I spent a morning in the medina, the heart of the city, getting lost in its maze of narrow alleyways. The medina is a place where the pulse of Tunisia beats most vibrantly. From the moment I entered, I was greeted by the sight of artisans weaving carpets, street vendors selling fragrant spices, and locals bargaining over everything from copperware to leather goods. The colors and scents of the market were overwhelming, but in the best way. There's something magical about a place that feels so alive, where the sounds of the street blend with the prayers of the call to mosque, echoing through the alleys. I wandered into a small shop that sold intricately embroidered fabrics and, as I admired the delicate threads, the shopkeeper offered me a cup of mint tea, an act of hospitality that would become a recurring theme throughout my journey in Tunisia. I soon learned that Tunisians take great pride in sharing their culture with visitors, and I was welcomed not just as a tourist but as a guest, treated with kindness and generosity every step of the way.

A short drive from Tunis took me to the ruins of Carthage, one of the most iconic archaeological sites in the Mediterranean. I stood in awe among the ancient ruins, pondering the rise and fall of one of the greatest empires of antiquity. The Punic and Roman remains, from the crumbling amphitheaters to the majestic temples, felt like whispers from a forgotten time. I walked through the Antonine Baths, imagining the grandeur that once existed here. Carthage, with its stunning views of the Mediterranean, is a place where the past is never too far from the present. Standing by the ruins, looking out at the sparkling sea, it was easy to understand why this city once held such power and influence. In Carthage, history isn't just something you read about in textbooks; it's something you feel in your bones as the winds of time sweep across the ancient stones.

From Carthage, I headed south to the town of Sousse, a coastal city known for its sandy beaches and historical medina. Here, the rhythm of life slowed down a bit, and I was able to take in the relaxed pace of Tunisia's seaside culture. Sousse's medina, a UNESCO World Heritage site, was a delightful labyrinth of winding streets, where I spent hours strolling and exploring. The town's 9th-century ribat, a fortress that once guarded Tunisia's coast, offered panoramic views of the town and the Mediterranean, and I marveled at how the fort's walls still stand strong, guarding the city as they have for centuries. At a small café overlooking the water, I had my first taste of traditional *brik*, a Tunisian pastry filled with egg and tuna, and sipped on fresh mint tea, the flavor still vivid in my memory. The warmth of the people, coupled with the beauty of the landscape, made Sousse a place that felt both timeless and serene.

My journey then took me to the historic city of Kairouan, a place that felt almost sacred. Kairouan is one of the holiest cities in Islam, and its Great Mosque, a masterpiece of Islamic architecture, was a highlight of my travels. As I walked through the mosque's vast courtyard, the serenity and the sense of history overwhelmed me. Kairouan is a city that invites reflection, and standing inside its ancient walls, it was easy to sense how deeply the city's culture and religion have shaped not just Tunisia, but the entire region. I spent the day exploring its tranquil streets, visiting small workshops where artisans create handwoven carpets and traditional leather goods. In Kairouan, the rhythms of daily life are inextricably tied to the city's religious and cultural traditions, and it was here that I felt the most connected to Tunisia's roots.

No journey through Tunisia would be complete without experiencing the Sahara Desert, and so I made my way to the southern town of Tozeur, a gateway to the vastness of the desert. The Sahara was everything I had imagined and more. It's a place where time seems to stretch, where the horizon seems endless, and where the silence is so profound that it becomes almost tangible. I took a camel trek into the dunes, guided by a local Berber who shared stories of the desert and its people. The ride through the vast, undulating sand dunes felt surreal—like a scene out of an ancient tale, the camel's rhythmic steps in sync with the beating of my own heart. As night fell, I stayed in a traditional desert camp, where the stars above shone brighter than any I had ever seen. Around the campfire, I was treated to music and stories by the locals, who spoke of life in the desert with a quiet reverence that resonated deeply within me. The desert, with its stark beauty and timelessness, had a profound effect on me. It felt as though I had been transported to another world, a world where the demands of daily life had faded away, leaving only the purity of the earth, the sky, and the stars.

One of the most memorable aspects of my journey was the incredible hospitality I encountered throughout Tunisia. From the moment I arrived, I felt welcomed, not as a tourist, but as a guest in people's homes and communities. I was invited into homes to share meals, offered directions by complete strangers, and greeted with kindness wherever I went. In Tozeur, a local family invited me to their home for a traditional Tunisian meal of couscous, lamb, and a variety of fresh vegetables. As we sat around the table, I learned about their lives, their history, and their hopes for the future. There was a sense of community, a shared understanding that hospitality is more than just a gesture—it's a way of life. This genuine warmth is something I'll always associate with Tunisia. It's a country where people take pride in sharing their culture, their food, and their stories, and where the lines between visitor and local seem to blur in the best possible way.

My travels through Tunisia were not just about seeing new places; they were about engaging with a rich culture, experiencing the profound connections that people have with their history, their land, and each other. Tunisia is a place where the past is deeply intertwined with the present, and where the warmth and hospitality of its people offer a rich and authentic experience for any traveler willing to immerse themselves in its culture. Every city, every town, and every interaction offered something new—a new perspective, a new understanding, a deeper connection to the country's soul. From the ancient ruins of Carthage to the sweeping dunes of the Sahara, from the bustling souks of Tunis to the quiet serenity of Kairouan, Tunisia is a land that will stay with me, offering layers of discovery long after my journey ended.

CHAPTER 1: TRIP PLANNING

When to Visit Tunisia

Tunisia is a country that can be visited year-round, but the best time to experience its full range of offerings largely depends on what you're looking for during your trip. The country's diverse geography, from Mediterranean coastlines to the arid Sahara Desert, means that different seasons present unique experiences. Whether you're in search of warm sunny days on the beach, exploring ancient ruins, or seeking adventure in the desert, understanding the seasonal shifts and the rhythm of Tunisia's festivals and events can greatly enhance your visit.

Tunisian summers, from June to August, are hot and dry, especially in the interior and southern parts of the country. The coastal cities, like Tunis, Hammamet, Sousse, and Monastir, offer a slightly milder climate due to the Mediterranean breeze, but it can still get uncomfortably warm for some travelers. The heat peaks in July and August, when temperatures can easily soar above 35°C (95°F) in the cities and much higher in the desert regions. While this is prime time for beachgoers, as the Mediterranean waters remain cool and refreshing, it's also the time when the country experiences its peak tourist season. Beaches are bustling, resorts are crowded, and the coastal cities come alive with festivals and cultural events. If you enjoy the lively atmosphere, lively seaside resorts, and don't mind the heat, summer could be an excellent choice. However, for those who prefer a quieter, more leisurely experience, the summer months may feel overwhelming.

If you're visiting for the cultural festivals, then the summer months are when you'll find many of Tunisia's most prominent events taking place. The Carthage Film Festival, usually held in late summer, attracts filmmakers from all over the Arab world and beyond. This international festival is an important cultural event and an excellent opportunity for movie buffs to see the latest in Arab and African cinema. Similarly, the International Festival of the Sahara in Tozeur, which typically occurs in late August, celebrates Tunisia's southern desert culture through music, dance, and traditional performances. This festival provides a deep dive into Tunisia's Berber roots and the cultural richness of its southern communities. During this time, visitors can expect a mix of desert performances, camel races, and exhibitions, making it a truly unique celebration of Tunisia's diverse cultural heritage.

Autumn, from September to November, is one of the most favorable seasons to visit Tunisia. Temperatures during this time are much more pleasant, especially for those wanting to explore Tunisia's historical sites and landscapes. With the summer heat behind you, the weather is ideal for both sightseeing and outdoor activities. The coastal regions still enjoy warm weather, making it perfect for swimming and relaxing on the beach, but the crowds are fewer compared to the high summer season. Cities like Tunis, Sousse, and Hammamet become more relaxed, and the Mediterranean breeze feels much more refreshing. Inland, the temperatures are cooler, making it easier to visit the ancient ruins of Dougga, El Djem, and Kairouan without the intense heat of the summer months. In the Sahara, autumn temperatures are still warm, but not excessively hot, offering a more comfortable climate for desert excursions.

Autumn is also the time when Tunisia's olive harvest begins, and visitors have the opportunity to see the olive groves in full production. Tunisia is one of the world's largest producers of olive oil, and during this season, travelers can visit rural farms to witness the traditional olive picking process. The sight of people working in the groves, the fresh scent of olives, and the chance to sample some of the finest olive oil in the world adds a special charm to the season.

The winter months, from December to February, are mild and can be a great time to experience Tunisia with fewer tourists. The temperatures along the coast are cool but not freezing, with average highs of around 15-18°C (59-64°F), which makes it an excellent time for sightseeing without the crowds of summer. The winter months are quieter, and visitors can explore Tunisia's cities, medinas, and ruins in peace. In the Sahara, however, temperatures can dip quite low at night, and it's essential to come prepared with warm clothing if you plan to experience a desert night under the stars. While it's not beach weather in the traditional sense, the winter months are an excellent time to visit historical sites like the ancient city of Carthage, the amphitheater of

El Djem, and the ruins of Dougga. These sites, often less crowded during winter, allow for more intimate exploration.

Winter is also a time when Tunisia holds some of its most cultural and religious celebrations. One of the most notable festivals is the Mouloud, which celebrates the birth of the Prophet Muhammad. The festival, which takes place in November or December, is marked by religious processions, prayers, and community gatherings. In many parts of the country, especially in cities like Kairouan, you'll find families coming together for communal meals, celebrating the event with traditional sweets and offerings. It's a great way for visitors to see the depth of Tunisia's Islamic heritage and its celebrations of religious milestones.

Spring, from March to May, is another fantastic time to visit Tunisia, as the weather is mild, and nature is in full bloom. The landscapes become lush and green, especially in the northern regions of the country, where the rainfalls turn the countryside into a vibrant display of wildflowers and greenery. This is the perfect time to visit Tunisia's national parks, such as Ichkeul National Park, a UNESCO World Heritage site, known for its beautiful wetlands and birdlife. Migratory birds flock to the park during the spring months, making it a haven for birdwatchers. The weather is comfortable, with daytime temperatures ranging from 20°C to 25°C (68°F to 77°F), ideal for outdoor activities like hiking or camel trekking in the desert.

Spring also offers the opportunity to experience the country's lively festivals and events. The International

Festival of the Medina in Tunis, held in April or May, is one such event that attracts both locals and tourists alike. The festival celebrates the rich cultural heritage of Tunisia through music, dance, and performances, held within the historic medina of Tunis. The air is filled with the sounds of traditional Tunisian music, and the streets come alive with the performances of local artists. Spring is also when the annual Olive Festival takes place in the town of Sfax, showcasing Tunisia's deep connection to its olive oil production.

The best time to visit Tunisia depends on your preferences for climate and the kind of experience you're looking for. If you enjoy the bustling atmosphere of summer festivals and beach holidays, then the summer months are ideal. However, for those who prefer milder temperatures, fewer crowds, and a more relaxed pace, autumn and spring are the most pleasant times to explore the country. Winter offers a unique, quieter experience, especially if you're looking to engage with Tunisia's cultural and religious traditions. Whatever the season, Tunisia has a variety of offerings, from its ancient history and vibrant culture to its stunning natural landscapes, making it a destination worth visiting at any time of the year.

Visa and Entry Informations

When planning a trip to Tunisia, understanding the visa and entry requirements is crucial to ensure a smooth and hassle-free arrival. While the process can vary depending on your nationality, there are several general guidelines that most travelers can follow to gain entry into this fascinating North African country. Tunisia's visa policies have been designed to streamline tourism and encourage visitors, but as with any international trip, it's important to familiarize yourself with the specific entry rules that apply to your situation.

For many nationalities, including citizens from the European Union, the United States, Canada, Australia, and several other countries, Tunisia offers visa-free entry for short stays, typically up to 90 days. This means that travelers from these countries do not need to apply for a visa before arriving in Tunisia for tourism or business purposes. However, there are a few important details to keep in mind even if you are exempt from a visa requirement. First, your passport should be valid for at least six months beyond your intended date of arrival in Tunisia. This is a common requirement for many international destinations, and it helps to ensure that travelers are not faced with any complications during their stay. Additionally, you should have a return or onward travel ticket, as authorities may request proof that you will leave the country within the allowed period.

If you are traveling from a country that requires a visa to enter Tunisia, you will need to apply for a tourist visa at a

Tunisian embassy or consulate in your home country or the country where you are residing. The tourist visa for Tunisia is typically issued for stays of up to 90 days, and the application process is relatively straightforward. To apply, you will need to submit several documents, including a valid passport, passport-sized photographs, a completed visa application form, proof of accommodation (such as hotel bookings or an invitation letter if you are staying with friends or relatives), and proof of sufficient funds to support your stay in Tunisia. It's also important to note that some nationalities may need to provide additional documents, such as a travel itinerary or a letter from an employer if visiting for business purposes. Processing times for a visa application can vary, but it's generally advisable to apply at least two to three weeks before your planned departure to allow enough time for processing.

If you are planning to visit Tunisia for purposes other than tourism, such as business or study, there are specific visa categories to consider. Business visas, for example, may require a letter from your employer or an invitation from a Tunisian company, along with additional documents that verify the purpose of your visit. Similarly, if you are going to Tunisia for educational purposes, you may need a student visa, for which you will need to provide an acceptance letter from a Tunisian institution and evidence of financial means to support your studies and living expenses.

In addition to the standard entry requirements, visitors to Tunisia may also be subject to health and safety regulations. As of recent years, travelers are sometimes asked to present proof of vaccination for certain diseases, particularly if coming from regions affected by outbreaks. It's a good idea to check the latest health advisory information on the Tunisian Ministry of Health website or consult with your local embassy for any specific health requirements or vaccinations recommended before travel. Depending on global circumstances, travelers might also need to adhere to temporary protocols related to health security, such as COVID-19 testing, quarantine measures, or health screening on arrival.

Upon arrival in Tunisia, all travelers must pass through immigration control at the airport or port of entry. Here, the border control officer will check your passport and any required documents, and they may ask questions regarding the purpose of your visit and your plans while in Tunisia. While the process is usually straightforward, it's always good practice to have all necessary documents prepared and easily accessible to avoid any delays. The officer may also ask for proof of sufficient funds to cover your stay, as well as your return ticket or onward travel arrangements.

In the case of travelers wishing to extend their stay beyond the initial 90 days allowed for visa-exempt countries, it is possible to apply for an extension at the nearest local police station or immigration office in Tunisia. Extensions are typically granted for an additional 30 to 60 days, but they are not guaranteed and must be requested before the initial 90-day period expires. For those on a tourist visa, the process is generally similar. However, it's important to note that overstaying your visa in Tunisia can result in fines or, in some cases, deportation. It's always advisable to ensure that your stay remains within the allowed time frame unless an extension is officially granted.

For those considering long-term stays, such as for work or residence, Tunisia also offers specific residence permits. These permits are usually issued for individuals who have secured a job or have business interests in the country. The application process for a long-term stay is more involved and will require proof of employment or other relevant documentation. It's highly recommended to seek assistance from a legal advisor or the Tunisian immigration office to understand the full requirements for long-term stays.

It's also worth mentioning that Tunisia is relatively flexible when it comes to entry and exit for travelers with special circumstances. For example, if you are arriving with a diplomatic passport or for official government business, different rules may apply, and in these cases, it is recommended to contact the nearest embassy or consulate for tailored guidance.

Entering Tunisia is a relatively simple process for most international visitors, with the ease of travel being one of the country's key attractions. The country's strategic position as a tourism hub in North Africa means that entry requirements are straightforward for a large number of nationalities. However, regardless of your nationality or the purpose of your visit, it's crucial to ensure that you meet the necessary criteria before embarking on your journey. Planning ahead by checking the specific visa requirements, ensuring that your passport is valid for the required length of time, and keeping abreast of any health or safety regulations will ensure that your trip to Tunisia begins smoothly, allowing you to focus on experiencing the country's rich history, culture, and landscapes without any unnecessary complications.

Money Matters: Currency, Exchange and More

Understanding the country's currency, exchange rates, and tipping etiquette can greatly enhance your experience, ensuring that you're well-prepared for daily expenses and interactions. Tunisia's financial system is fairly straightforward, but like any foreign destination, it's important to familiarize yourself with the local practices to avoid any confusion or surprises.

The official currency of Tunisia is the Tunisian Dinar (TND). It is important to note that the Tunisian dinar is a closed currency, meaning it cannot be exchanged outside the country. You will need to exchange your home currency into dinars either at a local bank or a licensed currency exchange office while you are in Tunisia. The currency itself comes in both banknotes and coins, with banknotes in denominations of 5, 10, 20, and 50 dinars, and coins in denominations of 1, 2, 5, 10, and 20 millimes (a millime is one-thousandth of a dinar, and while you may not encounter them often, they are still in circulation). The dinar is subdivided into 1,000 millimes, although in practice, millimes are used mostly for small change in everyday transactions, with most prices being quoted in whole dinars.

One of the first things visitors should know is that Tunisia has a relatively low cost of living compared to many Western countries. The exchange rate can vary depending on economic factors, but generally speaking, Tunisia offers good value for money when it comes to accommodation, food, and transportation. In recent years, the Tunisian dinar has tended to be weaker compared to major currencies such as the Euro, the US Dollar, and the British Pound. For example, as of recent exchange rates, 1 Euro is equivalent to about 3.20 Tunisian dinars, and 1 US Dollar equals around 3 TND, though fluctuations can occur. These rates can be checked regularly at local banks or currency exchange bureaus for up-to-date information. However, when planning a budget for your trip, it's wise to anticipate that currency exchange rates may shift, so it's always a good idea to keep an eye on these before converting a large sum of money.

There are various ways to exchange your money once in Tunisia. Banks are a reliable option, offering fair exchange rates and a secure environment for making transactions. Tunisia has a number of local banks that cater to tourists, and they can be found in most major cities and tourist hotspots. Keep in mind, however, that banks may charge a small fee for currency exchange, and they often close for lunch, so planning ahead is recommended. In addition to banks, there are many currency exchange offices, especially in tourist areas like Tunis, Sousse, Hammamet, and Djerba, where you can easily swap your currency. While these offices typically offer competitive rates, it's still a good idea to shop around a little to make sure you're getting a fair deal. ATMs are also widely available in major towns and cities, allowing you to withdraw local currency directly from your bank account, though international withdrawals often incur a fee, so it's important to check with your home bank about any charges before you travel.

Credit cards are accepted in many hotels, larger restaurants, and stores, particularly in tourist-heavy areas, but they are not as commonly used in smaller, more rural areas. Visa and MasterCard are the most widely accepted, while American Express and other cards may not be as easily usable. For the most part, it's a good idea to carry a sufficient amount of cash with you, especially when traveling to smaller towns, remote areas, or markets, where card payments may not be an option. When paying with cash, make sure to have small denominations, as many places may not have enough change for larger bills.

For those looking to manage their expenses, Tunisia remains a relatively affordable destination. Food, particularly street food and meals at local restaurants, is generally inexpensive. Traditional Tunisian dishes such as *couscous*, *brik* (fried pastries with egg and tuna), and *mechoui* (roasted lamb) are all widely available at very reasonable prices, often in the range of 5 to 15 dinars for a meal. In more tourist-centric areas or upscale restaurants, prices will be higher, but still typically lower than in Western countries. Local markets (souks) also offer great bargains for handcrafted items, spices, and textiles, although negotiating is expected, and can be a fun part of the experience.

When it comes to tipping etiquette, Tunisia follows a fairly relaxed but customary approach. Tipping is not obligatory, but it is appreciated, especially in the tourism and hospitality sectors, where it is often a significant part of workers' income. In general, tips are small but meaningful. In restaurants, it's common to leave around 5 to 10% of the total bill if the service was satisfactory, but it's not mandatory. In some cases, especially in more casual eateries or cafés, rounding up the bill or leaving a small amount of change is perfectly acceptable. In larger or more tourist-oriented restaurants, a 5 to 10 dinar tip for good service is a nice gesture, though if the service charge is already included in the bill, additional tipping is not required unless you feel the service warrants it.

Tipping in hotels is also common, particularly for bellboys, housekeepers, and porters. A small tip of 1 to 5 dinars per service is generally appreciated. When using taxis, rounding up the fare or leaving an additional 1 to 2 dinars is customary, though in larger cities, such as Tunis or Sousse, drivers may not expect a large tip unless they've gone out of their way to provide extra assistance, such as helping with luggage or providing guidance.

Guides and tour operators are another category where tipping is customary. For a half-day tour, a tip of around 10 to 20 dinars per person is generally appreciated, depending on the level of service and the tour experience. If you've hired a private guide for a full-day excursion, a tip of 20 to 30 dinars would be a thoughtful way to express your satisfaction. The same applies to drivers for private transport or longer journeys, who typically expect a tip of around 10 to 20 dinars.

In some more traditional or rural settings, tipping might not be as frequent, and you may not encounter it as often, but it's still a kind gesture that is welcomed. While not all services in Tunisia demand tips, and there are certainly places where no gratuity is expected, offering a small tip shows appreciation for service and helps foster goodwill with local workers. Additionally, always remember to give tips directly to the person who provided the service, as it's considered more personal and respectful than leaving money on a table or in a tip box.

For larger purchases or transactions in shops and markets, tipping is not necessary unless you feel that extra attention or assistance was provided. Some visitors may choose to tip for particularly attentive or helpful service, especially in tourist areas, but generally, tipping for shopping purchases is not a norm.

In Tunisia, as in many other countries, attitudes toward tipping can vary. While it's not an absolute necessity, being considerate and recognizing good service through tipping can go a long way in building positive interactions with the local population. Visitors should be mindful of the local customs and approach tipping with respect, understanding that even small gestures can be seen as acts of kindness and appreciation.

Tunisia's currency, exchange rates, and tipping etiquette offer a relatively straightforward system for visitors to navigate. With a little planning ahead regarding currency exchange, and understanding the customary approach to tipping, you'll be able to manage your finances while also engaging with local culture in a respectful and considerate manner.

Health and Safety Tips

While Tunisia is generally a safe destination for tourists, it is important to take proactive steps to protect yourself from any potential health risks and understand the healthcare system in the country. From securing travel insurance to being aware of vaccinations, and knowing how to navigate the local healthcare services, there are a number of considerations that will help you prepare for a smooth and enjoyable visit.

One of the most important first steps when preparing for a trip abroad is securing travel insurance. Travel insurance is essential because it covers a wide range of potential issues that could arise during your trip, from minor inconveniences to serious emergencies. For example, should you encounter an illness, an accident, or a sudden medical emergency, travel insurance can cover medical expenses, hospital stays, emergency evacuation, and even repatriation if necessary. Health care services in Tunisia, especially in major cities like Tunis, Sousse, and Hammamet, are generally of good quality, but private medical care can be expensive for foreign visitors without insurance. The cost of medical treatment, particularly if you require surgery, hospitalization, or treatment for a chronic condition, can quickly add up. Thus, a comprehensive travel insurance policy that includes medical coverage will offer peace of mind and help you avoid unexpected financial burdens in the event of an emergency.

In addition to medical coverage, travel insurance can also provide protection for trip cancellations, delays, or lost baggage, making it an invaluable safety net for a variety of unforeseen circumstances. For those traveling to Tunisia, especially for extended periods or on an adventure, it's important to select a policy that includes coverage for activities you plan to engage in, whether it's hiking, desert excursions, or water sports. Checking with your insurance provider to confirm that your coverage applies to the specific activities you will be doing is always a wise move.

Beyond travel insurance, vaccinations are another key element of preparing for your trip to Tunisia. While the country does not have any mandatory vaccination requirements for most travelers, it's highly recommended to ensure you are up to date on routine vaccinations before departure. Routine vaccinations include those for measles, mumps, rubella, polio, and diphtheria, tetanus, and pertussis (DTaP). In addition to these, travelers to Tunisia are often advised to get vaccines for hepatitis A, hepatitis B, typhoid, and rabies, especially if you plan to visit rural areas or engage in activities that could expose you to animal bites or food and waterborne illnesses. Vaccines for diseases like influenza (flu) may also be beneficial, particularly if you're traveling during the winter months.

Hepatitis A and typhoid are particularly important for travelers, as both are transmitted through contaminated food or water. Hepatitis A vaccination is especially recommended for anyone planning to eat in local restaurants, street food stalls, or anywhere where food hygiene may be a concern. Typhoid fever is also common in some parts of Tunisia, so getting vaccinated before your trip can help mitigate the risk of contracting the disease.

While there is no specific malaria risk in Tunisia, travelers planning to visit rural areas or the Sahara Desert may want to consider taking additional precautions against mosquito bites, particularly if traveling during the warmer months when mosquitoes are more prevalent. Using insect repellent containing DEET, wearing long sleeves and pants, and sleeping under a mosquito net can all help reduce the risk of being bitten.

For those traveling with children or infants, it's important to ensure that their vaccinations are up to date, and consult with a healthcare provider about additional immunizations specific to travel in North Africa. Infants and young children may be at a higher risk for certain illnesses, so taking extra precautions can provide significant protection.

Aside from vaccinations, health advice for Tunisia also includes being mindful of food and water safety. While Tunisia has modern infrastructure, the quality of food and water can vary, especially outside of major cities or in less developed areas. It's advisable to drink bottled water throughout your stay, as tap water may not be treated to the same standards as what you're accustomed to at home. This is especially true in rural areas or more remote regions, where water sanitation may be less reliable. Additionally, avoid ice in drinks unless you are sure it is made from bottled or purified water.

Food hygiene is another consideration, particularly if you plan to sample street food, which is often delicious but may not always meet the same health standards as food prepared in higher-end restaurants. Choose food vendors who appear clean and busy, as these are typically indicators of better food safety practices. If you have a sensitive stomach, it's a good idea to stick to cooked food, avoid raw fruits and vegetables unless they are peeled, and ensure that meat is thoroughly cooked. Be cautious with dairy products, especially if they are unpasteurized, as they can be a source of bacterial contamination.

In case of illness or injury, Tunisia's healthcare system is generally capable of dealing with most medical needs. The major cities, particularly Tunis, Sousse, and Hammamet, have both public and private hospitals that provide modern medical care, with private hospitals often offering better services for foreign visitors. English is widely spoken in the healthcare sector, especially in private hospitals, so language barriers should not be a significant issue. However, in more rural or remote areas, you may find that medical staff are less proficient in foreign languages, so learning a few basic phrases in Arabic or French (the official languages of Tunisia) can be helpful.

If you do fall ill or sustain an injury, you can visit a pharmacy, as they are abundant throughout Tunisia and are usually well-stocked with over-the-counter medications. Many pharmacists are knowledgeable and can offer advice on common ailments like colds, stomach upsets, and minor injuries. However, for more serious conditions, it's important to seek medical treatment at a hospital or clinic.

In the case of a medical emergency, you can dial 190 for an ambulance, though response times can vary, especially in more rural areas.

For travelers with pre-existing medical conditions, it's essential to plan ahead. Carry enough medication to last the duration of your stay, as not all medications may be readily available in Tunisia. It's also a good idea to carry a doctor's note or prescription, particularly if you need to bring controlled substances or any medication that could be restricted in Tunisia. Be aware that some medications available in your home country may not be legally available in Tunisia, so it's crucial to check the specifics of what you can bring before your trip.

By securing comprehensive travel insurance, staying updated on recommended vaccinations, following food and water safety guidelines, and understanding the local healthcare options, you can ensure that your trip to Tunisia is as safe and enjoyable as possible. Being prepared allows you to focus on experiencing the rich culture, history, and landscapes of Tunisia, confident that you've taken the necessary steps to protect your health and well-being during your travels.

Packing Guide

The country's diverse geography and climate, ranging from the Mediterranean coast to the Sahara Desert, mean that what you pack will depend not only on the season but also on the activities you plan to undertake. Whether you're exploring the historic ruins, relaxing on the beach, or trekking through the dunes, it's important to pack wisely so that you can fully enjoy the country's rich offerings without being weighed down by unnecessary items.

A key consideration when packing for Tunisia is the climate. Tunisia's weather varies significantly depending on the season and the region. Along the coast, the weather is typically Mediterranean, with hot summers and mild, wet winters. The interior of the country and the Sahara Desert experience more extreme temperatures, with scorching summers and cooler winters. Therefore, it's advisable to pack for both hot and cooler conditions, especially if your trip involves traveling across different regions.

In the summer months (from June to September), temperatures along the coast can soar above 30°C (86°F), while inland and in the desert, temperatures can climb even higher, reaching 40°C (104°F) or more. In these conditions, lightweight, breathable clothing is a must. You'll want to pack clothing that is made from natural fabrics like cotton or linen, which are breathable and comfortable in the heat. Opt for loose-fitting clothes that allow air to circulate around your body, helping you stay cool in the high temperatures. Long sleeves and long pants can offer extra protection against the sun, particularly when venturing into the desert. Tunisia is a conservative country, especially in more rural or traditional areas, so it's respectful to dress modestly. While you won't need to cover your entire body, it's a good idea to avoid overly revealing outfits. For women, a simple scarf or shawl can be useful for covering the shoulders when visiting religious sites or more conservative areas.

In terms of footwear, comfortable, durable shoes are essential for exploring Tunisia, especially if you plan to do any walking tours or visit ancient ruins. A pair of sturdy sandals or comfortable walking shoes will be invaluable. If you're planning to visit the desert, you may want to bring lightweight but sturdy boots or shoes with closed toes to protect your feet from the hot sand and any sharp rocks. For beachgoers, flip-flops or water shoes are ideal, as they'll keep you comfortable and protected while enjoying the coastal areas.

When packing for Tunisia, also consider the possibility of cooler evenings, particularly in the desert or in more inland areas, where temperatures can drop significantly once the sun sets. A light jacket or sweater will help keep you warm during these times. In winter, temperatures along the coast remain mild, but in the desert, it can get quite chilly. A heavier jacket, especially for evening outings, will help keep you warm if you're visiting Tunisia during the cooler months (from December to February). If you're traveling to higher altitudes or places like the Atlas Mountains, you might also want to pack a fleece or a light down jacket to stay comfortable in cooler climates.

For sunscreen, it's essential to pack a high SPF to protect your skin from the strong sun, particularly if you'll be spending a lot of time outdoors, whether exploring ancient sites, hiking, or lounging on the beach. Tunisia has long, sunny days, especially in the summer, and sunburn can occur quickly. Don't forget a good pair of sunglasses with UV protection to shield your eyes from the bright sun. A wide-brimmed hat can also be beneficial, providing shade for your face and helping keep you cool in the desert heat.

You'll also want to be prepared for the practicalities of travel in Tunisia. A reliable daypack or backpack is crucial for carrying your essentials, especially if you plan on taking day trips to historical sites or traveling by public transport. The bag should be lightweight but large enough to hold a water bottle, sunscreen, camera, and other personal items. Many tourists in Tunisia find themselves walking long distances, especially when exploring ancient ruins like the Roman amphitheater in El Djem or the medina in Tunis, so a comfortable, easy-to-carry bag is vital.

Speaking of water, hydration is crucial in Tunisia, especially in the warmer months. Be sure to pack a reusable water bottle that you can refill throughout the day. It's important to avoid drinking tap water, so bottled water is readily available throughout the country. However, having your own bottle can save you money and reduce plastic waste.

If you plan to swim or spend time at the beach, pack appropriate swimwear. While Tunisia is relatively liberal when it comes to swimwear at resorts and beaches, remember that modesty is appreciated in some areas, particularly in rural or conservative regions. It's common to wear a cover-up or something more modest when walking to and from the beach.

For your electronics, bring the appropriate adapters and voltage converters if necessary. Tunisia uses a 230V supply voltage and a plug type C (two-round-pronged plugs), so make sure your devices are compatible. If you're traveling with a camera, phone, or tablet, also bring extra memory cards, chargers, and a power bank, as you may find that electricity outages or limited access to charging stations are occasional occurrences in some remote areas. For photographers, you'll want to pack a camera with a good zoom lens for capturing Tunisia's stunning landscapes and ancient ruins. A waterproof case for your phone or camera is also a great idea if you plan to do any activities near the water.

For health and hygiene, packing a basic first aid kit is always wise. This should include essential items like pain relievers, antiseptic wipes, band-aids, and any prescription medications you may need. If you have any pre-existing medical conditions, ensure you bring enough medication to last the duration of your trip, along with any necessary documentation from your doctor. Many pharmacies in Tunisia are well-stocked and can provide over-the-counter medication for minor ailments, but it's always good to have your own supplies, especially if you're traveling to more remote areas. You'll also want to pack toiletries like toothpaste, toothbrush, soap, and shampoo. While these items are widely available in Tunisia, you may prefer to bring your own, particularly if you have specific preferences or skin sensitivities.

For those who plan to shop during their visit, Tunisia offers a variety of locally made goods, from artisan crafts and textiles to spices and jewelry. It's a good idea to leave some extra space in your luggage for any souvenirs you may want to bring home. When visiting local markets (souks), consider carrying small change for purchases, as haggling is common, and being able to pay with exact money can often simplify the process.

In addition to personal items, consider packing a few travel accessories that will make your trip more comfortable. A good travel pillow can be useful for long journeys, especially if you're traveling by bus or train to different regions. A lightweight, foldable shopping bag can also come in handy for carrying extra items when you're exploring local markets or purchasing snacks and drinks. Also, bring a travel lock or a small portable safe to keep valuables secure in your hotel room, as a precaution against theft.

Packing for Tunisia requires a balance of preparation for the hot, sunny days and cooler nights, as well as for exploring the diverse landscapes the country offers. With a thoughtful selection of clothing, accessories, and essentials, you'll be well-equipped to navigate the country's vibrant culture, bustling markets, and historic sites with ease, ensuring that your trip to Tunisia is as comfortable and enjoyable as possible.

Getting to Tunisia

Flights to Tunisia are relatively accessible from various regions, with the country served by several international airports that cater to a diverse range of travelers. Whether you're coming from Europe, the Middle East, or beyond, there are plenty of flight options to get you to this fascinating North African destination. Tunisia is well-connected by air, with flights arriving in major cities such as Tunis, Enfidha, and Monastir, offering both direct and connecting routes to accommodate travelers.

The main international airport in Tunisia is **Tunis-Carthage International Airport** (IATA: TUN), located approximately 8 kilometers (5 miles) from the center of the capital city, Tunis. The airport serves as the primary gateway for international travelers and is the hub for Tunisia's national airline, **Tunisair**. Tunis-Carthage handles flights from Europe, the Middle East, and a number of destinations within Africa, as well as seasonal routes from various parts of the world. The airport is well-equipped with modern facilities, including duty-free shops, restaurants, lounges, and currency exchange services, making it a comfortable point of entry for visitors.

In addition to Tunis-Carthage, **Monastir Habib Bourguiba International Airport** (IATA: MIR) is another important entry point for travelers to Tunisia, particularly for those heading to the eastern part of the country. Located about 8 kilometers (5 miles) from the city center of Monastir, the airport is a popular choice for tourists visiting resorts along the coast in areas like Sousse, Hammamet, and the island of Djerba. Monastir Habib Bourguiba International Airport is well-connected to several European cities, and its proximity to popular beach resorts makes it a convenient choice for visitors seeking a more relaxed, resort-style vacation. The airport is named after Tunisia's first president, Habib Bourguiba, and offers various services including transportation to nearby destinations, duty-free shopping, and several restaurants.

A third key airport in Tunisia is **Enfidha-Hammamet International Airport** (IATA: NBE), located about 40 kilometers (25 miles) from the popular tourist areas of Hammamet and Sousse. Enfidha Airport serves as a seasonal hub for charter flights and low-cost carriers, particularly during the summer months when tourist traffic peaks. This airport is a great choice for travelers heading to the eastern coastal areas or those planning to visit Tunisia's Mediterranean beaches. It offers a range of amenities including restaurants, baggage services, and car rental options, but being a smaller airport, it may have fewer facilities than Tunis-Carthage or Monastir.

For those heading to the island of **Djerba**, **Djerba-Zarzis International Airport** (IATA: DJE) is the main airport serving the island. Located approximately 9 kilometers (5.5 miles) from the island's capital, Houmt Souk, Djerba-Zarzis is an important entry point for those visiting the island's beach resorts and historical sites. While the airport is smaller than Tunis-Carthage, it offers essential services like restaurants, currency exchange, and taxis, and serves several European routes, especially during the high summer season.

Flights to Tunisia are well-served by both full-service airlines and low-cost carriers, with the most prominent being **Tunisair**, the national airline of Tunisia. Tunisair operates a wide range of international flights connecting Tunisia to major cities across Europe, the Middle East, and North Africa. The airline offers direct flights to Tunis from destinations such as Paris, Rome, Frankfurt, Brussels, London, and Dubai. Tunisair also serves a number of domestic routes, connecting Tunis with cities like Monastir, Sousse, and Djerba. While Tunisair provides a good level of service, there are also several international airlines that operate flights to Tunisia, including **Air France**, **Alitalia**, **Lufthansa**, **British Airways**, **Turkish Airlines**, and **Emirates**, making it easy to find a convenient flight.

For budget-conscious travelers, **low-cost carriers** like **Ryanair**, **easyJet**, and **Transavia** operate seasonal and year-round flights from various European cities to Tunis, Monastir, and Enfidha. These airlines often offer cheaper fares, particularly if you book in advance or are flexible with your travel dates. Many of these budget airlines provide flights from major European hubs like London, Milan, Paris, and Barcelona, catering to travelers looking for affordable routes to Tunisia's most popular destinations. However, it's worth noting that low-cost carriers often charge for checked baggage, seat selection, and other services, so it's important to factor these additional costs into your overall travel budget.

The **average cost** of flights to Tunisia varies significantly based on your departure location, the time of year, and how far in advance you book. For example, flights from major

European cities like Paris, Rome, or London to Tunis typically range from $100 to $300 USD for a round-trip ticket if booked in advance. Prices can be significantly higher during the peak tourist season, particularly from June to September when demand is highest. For travelers flying from North America or further afield, flights to Tunisia are more expensive, with round-trip fares from the United States or Canada typically ranging from $600 to $1,200 USD, depending on the route and season.

The **distance** between Tunisia and key global cities varies depending on the starting point. For instance, the distance from Paris to Tunis is approximately 1,300 kilometers (810 miles), while from London to Tunis it's about 1,600 kilometers (1,000 miles). Flights from New York City to Tunis are around 7,800 kilometers (4,800 miles), taking approximately 9 to 10 hours of flight time. The distance from Dubai to Tunis is roughly 5,200 kilometers (3,200 miles), which takes about 7 to 8 hours of flight time.

When booking flights to Tunisia, it's important to take into account the **seasonal variations** in flight availability and pricing. The peak tourist season in Tunisia is during the summer months (June to September), when the weather is hottest, and many international tourists flock to the beaches and historical sites. During this time, flights can be more expensive and crowded, so booking early is advised to secure the best prices. In contrast, the shoulder seasons (spring and fall) offer more moderate temperatures and slightly lower prices for flights, making these months an excellent choice for travelers who want to avoid the summer crowds. Winter (December to February) is the low season for tourism, and while temperatures can be cool, especially in the northern regions, you'll often find cheaper flights and fewer crowds, particularly for those who plan to visit Tunisia's inland regions or historical sites.

For **arrivals at Tunis-Carthage**, the airport is well-equipped to handle international travelers, with customs and immigration facilities to process arriving passengers efficiently. Visitors arriving at the airport can access taxis and shuttle services that will take them to the city center or surrounding areas. It's recommended to use official taxis or private transport services arranged in advance, especially for a smooth transfer from the airport. In general, taxis in Tunisia do not have meters, so it's essential to agree on a fare with the driver before starting the journey to avoid confusion.

For passengers arriving at **Monastir** or **Enfidha**, transportation options include taxis, private transfers, or rental cars. Both airports are conveniently located near major resort towns and coastal areas, making it easy to reach your destination within 30 minutes to an hour after arrival. Public buses and shared transport options are also available, particularly from Enfidha, which serves many travelers headed for the beach resorts along the Mediterranean coast.

Booking a **return flight** from Tunisia back to your home country is straightforward, with many international airlines offering direct flights from Tunis-Carthage, Monastir, or Djerba to a variety of international destinations. Depending on the airline and route, you can often find affordable one-way tickets back to Europe or the Middle East, with return fares averaging around $100 to $400 USD for European routes.

Flights to Tunisia are relatively affordable and accessible from many parts of the world, with a variety of options depending on your departure city and travel preferences. Whether you're flying with a full-service carrier or a budget airline, the country's international airports are well-equipped to welcome you, ensuring a smooth start to your Tunisian adventure. Understanding your flight options, choosing the right season for travel, and considering transportation from the airport will help make your journey to Tunisia seamless and enjoyable.

CHAPTER 2: MUST-VISIT DESTINATIONS

Tunis & the Medina

Tunis, the capital city of Tunisia, is a vibrant blend of modernity and history, where contemporary life seamlessly intertwines with the remnants of a rich and varied past. At the heart of Tunis lies the **Medina**, a UNESCO World Heritage site that serves as the cultural and historical heart of the country. The Medina is a labyrinth of narrow alleys, bustling souks, traditional mosques, and ancient buildings, offering a glimpse into Tunisia's Islamic, Roman, and colonial history. A visit to Tunis and its Medina is an essential part of experiencing the country's rich cultural heritage, offering a mix of historical sites, local crafts, religious landmarks, and an immersive shopping experience.

The **Medina of Tunis** is located in the heart of the city, making it easily accessible by foot, taxi, or public transport. Once you arrive in Tunis, the Medina is just a short distance from the city's modern districts, and it is well connected by local taxis, buses, or even the light rail system. If you are staying in central Tunis, you can easily walk to the Medina from most major hotels. Visitors often enter through one of the many gates that still stand today, such as **Bab el-Bhar** (also known as the Porte de France), which is the main entrance to the Medina from the coastal area, or **Bab Jedid**, another significant gate near the historic city center. The Medina itself is a maze of winding streets, so it's advisable to take a local guide or to follow the signs for major attractions to ensure you don't miss anything.

Once inside, the **Medina** offers an abundance of historical landmarks and sites to explore, most of which are easily reachable on foot. One of the most prominent and iconic sites is the **Zitouna Mosque**, which is not only a major place of worship but also an important symbol of Islamic architecture in Tunisia. Established in the 8th century, the mosque is the largest in Tunis and holds immense religious and historical significance. While non-Muslim visitors cannot enter the mosque itself, the surrounding areas are worth visiting, and the mosque's towering minaret offers a great photo opportunity. The mosque is open to worshipers during prayer times, and the nearby courtyard offers visitors a sense of the grandeur of Islamic architecture, with its lush greenery and beautiful arches. Entry to the area surrounding the mosque is free, but if you wish to visit the museum adjacent to it or take a guided tour, a small fee is usually charged.

Another important site in the Medina is the **Dar Ben Abdallah Museum**, a historical house that has been transformed into a museum showcasing traditional Tunisian life and culture. The museum provides an insight into the architecture, daily life, and customs of Tunisian aristocracy during the 18th century. With its stunning courtyards, intricate tile work, and ornate ceilings, the Dar Ben Abdallah Museum is a visual treat. The museum is open every day except Mondays, usually from 9 AM to 5 PM, with an entry fee of about 5 TND (Tunisian Dinars) for adults. The museum's exhibits include traditional clothing, jewelry, furniture, and everyday objects, offering a window into the domestic life of a bygone era.

The **Medina** also features several historic **madrasas** (Islamic schools), such as the **Medersa el-Alioua**, which dates back to the 17th century. These madrasas are fascinating to visit for those interested in Islamic education, architecture, and the intellectual history of Tunisia. Some madrasas are still used for educational purposes, while others have been converted into museums or cultural centers. While entry to many madrasas is free, some charge a small fee for entry, and their opening times vary depending on their status as active places of worship or study.

One of the must-see sites for history enthusiasts is the **Bardo Museum**, located just outside the Medina in central Tunis. The museum is home to one of the most extensive collections of Roman mosaics in the world, showcasing the country's Roman past and the grandeur of ancient Carthage. The Bardo Museum also contains exhibits related to Tunisia's history during the Arab-Islamic period and beyond, offering a comprehensive overview of the country's cultural evolution. The museum is open every day except Monday, typically from 9 AM to 5 PM, and the entry fee is around 12 TND. The museum's extensive collection includes artifacts from Tunisia's diverse past, from prehistoric times to the Ottoman period.

Beyond the historical sites, the Medina of Tunis is famous for its **souks**—traditional marketplaces that have been operating for centuries. The souks in Tunis are filled with the scents of spices, perfumes, and leather goods, and they are a bustling hive of activity where you can shop for everything from **carpets** and **jewelry** to **textiles** and **handcrafted pottery**. The main souks are located in the northern part of the Medina, and each section specializes in a different craft. The **Souk El Attarine** is the place to go for perfumes, while the **Souk El Kouatnia** specializes in **gold and silver jewelry**. The **Souk El Fekka** is dedicated to leather goods, where visitors can find finely crafted bags, belts, and shoes. The souks are a great place to practice haggling, as bargaining is an expected part of the shopping experience in Tunisia.

Shopping in the Medina is an immersive experience, as you will likely find yourself weaving through narrow alleys lined with stalls and small shops. Don't be afraid to engage with the vendors—while bargaining can be intense, it is all part of the fun and culture of the Medina. Visitors are often given a warm welcome by the local shopkeepers, and it's common to be invited into their shops to admire their goods. While most of the shops are open daily from around 9 AM to 7 PM, the best time to visit is in the morning when the Medina is less crowded, and the shops are freshly stocked.

In addition to the Medina, the city of Tunis offers visitors many other attractions, including the **Carthage ruins** located just a short drive from the city. The ruins of ancient Carthage, once a powerful city-state and rival to Rome, are a must-visit for anyone interested in Tunisia's ancient history. The site includes the remnants of Roman baths, temples, and the famous Punic ports.

For a more modern perspective on Tunis, visitors can explore **Avenue Habib Bourguiba**, the city's main boulevard, which is lined with cafes, shops, and theaters, and often referred to as the "Champs-Élysées" of Tunis. This avenue offers a contrast to the ancient Medina, showcasing the modern, cosmopolitan side of the city with beautiful French colonial architecture.

When visiting the Medina and the surrounding historic sites, it's important to keep a few practical tips in mind. While the area is generally safe for tourists, the narrow streets can sometimes be confusing to navigate, and it's easy to get lost. Consider hiring a local guide, as they can offer valuable insights into the history of the Medina and help you navigate the maze of streets more efficiently. It's also wise to dress modestly, as Tunisia is a conservative Muslim country, and dressing respectfully will ensure you are comfortable and well-received.

The Medina of Tunis is also a place where you can enjoy the local food. Street food is a significant part of the cultural experience, and you'll find vendors selling **boreks** (pastry filled with meat or cheese), **couscous**, and **tagine**, alongside fresh juices and sweets like **baklava** and **makroud**. The cafes in and around the Medina serve traditional Tunisian coffee and mint tea, offering a perfect break after a few hours of sightseeing and shopping.

Tunis and its Medina offer an unforgettable experience for travelers interested in history, culture, and shopping. With its historic mosques, palaces, museums, and vibrant souks, the Medina serves as a window into the heart of Tunisia's past and present. Whether you're exploring ancient ruins, admiring the intricate architecture, bargaining for local handicrafts, or simply soaking in the atmosphere, a visit to Tunis and the Medina is an essential part of understanding the rich heritage of this North African gem.

Carthage

Carthage, one of the most iconic and historically significant sites in Tunisia, is a treasure trove of ancient ruins and cultural heritage that offers visitors a glimpse into the grandeur of a civilization long past. Once the heart of the Carthaginian Empire, Carthage was a powerful city-state and a major rival to Rome. The ruins that remain today stand as a testament to Carthage's wealth, influence, and sophisticated culture, and the archaeological sites spread across the hills of the city offer a fascinating journey through history. Visiting Carthage is an essential part of any trip to Tunisia, particularly for history enthusiasts and those interested in exploring ancient Mediterranean civilizations.

Located just 15 kilometers (9 miles) northeast of Tunis, Carthage is easily accessible by public transportation, taxi, or private car. The area is situated along the coast of the Mediterranean, offering visitors a beautiful combination of ancient ruins and scenic views over the sea. To get there from the city center of Tunis, you can take a local train from the **Tunis Marine Station**, which runs regularly and takes about 20 minutes to reach the **Carthage - Byrsa** station, a key point of entry for visitors to the archaeological sites. Taxis are also a convenient option, and they are readily available in Tunis; the ride will take around 20-30 minutes, depending on traffic. For those staying in the nearby coastal town of **Sidi Bou Said**, a charming village famous for its white and blue houses, Carthage is within walking distance, making it an ideal day trip from there.

Carthage's vast archaeological complex is spread over several key sites, each offering unique insights into the city's past. One of the most famous landmarks in Carthage is the **Byrsa Hill**, which offers panoramic views of the surrounding areas, including the Mediterranean Sea and the nearby city of Tunis. Byrsa Hill was the heart of ancient Carthage, and the ruins of the ancient city can be explored here, including the remains of the **Carthaginian Palace** and the **Carthage Museum**, which houses a vast collection of artifacts excavated from the site. The Carthage Museum itself is housed in a beautiful building that blends into the landscape, and its exhibits include ancient pottery, sculptures, inscriptions, and other artifacts that shed light on Carthaginian life. The museum is open daily from 9 AM to 5 PM, with an entry fee of about 12 Tunisian Dinars (TND). The museum is a must-visit for anyone wanting to understand the scope and significance of the Carthaginian civilization.

Another prominent attraction in Carthage is the **Antonine Baths**, one of the largest Roman baths in the world. The ruins of the Antonine Baths stand as a reminder of

Carthage's incorporation into the Roman Empire after its defeat in the Punic Wars. The bath complex was constructed in the 2nd century AD and covers an extensive area with beautifully preserved structures, including grand columns, mosaics, and massive pools. Visitors can wander through the vast open spaces of the ruins and imagine what it would have been like to visit the luxurious baths during the Roman era. Entry to the Antonine Baths costs about 10 TND, and the site is open daily from 9 AM to 5 PM.

One of the most famous archaeological sites in Carthage is the **Tophet**, an ancient cemetery that was used for the burial of infants. The Tophet has been the subject of much scholarly debate, as it is believed to have been used by the Carthaginians for religious rituals, including child sacrifices to their gods. The site contains hundreds of stelae (stone markers) with inscriptions and images, which have been partially deciphered to reveal the names and offerings dedicated to the gods. While the practice of child sacrifice remains controversial, the Tophet provides an intriguing glimpse into Carthaginian religion and beliefs. The site is open to visitors and is free of charge. It's located near the beach, making it a peaceful and thought-provoking place to visit.

Visitors to Carthage can also explore the remains of **Carthaginian harbors**, which were once among the most advanced in the ancient Mediterranean world. The two harbors—**the commercial harbor** and **the military harbor**—were strategically located to control Mediterranean trade routes and ensure Carthage's naval superiority. Today, the remains of these harbors include ancient docks, warehouses, and quays, some of which are still visible along the coastline. The harbors provide insight into the commercial and military might of the Carthaginian Empire and its ability to dominate Mediterranean trade. Visitors can take a walking tour along the waterfront and appreciate the scale of the harbor system, though there are few remains to see directly, as much of it is underwater.

Another important site is the **Carthage Amphitheater**, located near the Antonine Baths. The amphitheater, which could hold up to 30,000 spectators, was used for gladiatorial games, public executions, and other forms of entertainment during the Roman period. Today, the amphitheater is an open-air site with significant portions of the seating area and the stage still visible. While not as well-preserved as some other Roman theaters in Tunisia, the amphitheater offers an atmospheric setting for understanding the role of entertainment and public life in ancient Carthage.

For those with an interest in the more modern side of Carthage, the **Carthage National Museum** is another important cultural institution. Located in the modern district of Carthage, this museum focuses on the history of the city from its founding to its role under Roman rule and beyond. The museum is housed in an attractive building and has a comprehensive collection that includes ceramics, sculptures, and everyday items from different periods of Carthaginian and Roman history. It is open daily and has an entry fee of about 8 TND.

While Carthage's ruins are the main draw for most visitors, the surrounding area, with its lovely Mediterranean views and proximity to the charming town of **Sidi Bou Said**, offers an additional layer of appeal. Sidi Bou Said, with its characteristic white and blue-painted buildings, narrow cobblestone streets, and vibrant art scene, is a favorite spot for both tourists and locals. Many visitors to Carthage choose to spend some time exploring Sidi Bou Said as well, enjoying the cafes, art galleries, and beautiful gardens. The area is particularly well-known for its peaceful atmosphere and is a great place to relax after a day of exploring the ruins.

As for the practical aspects of visiting Carthage, it is important to plan for a full day to properly explore the area, especially if you intend to visit several of the archaeological sites. The heat can be intense, particularly in the summer months, so visitors should bring plenty of water, wear comfortable shoes, and take breaks as needed. It is also advisable to carry sunscreen and a hat, as much of the exploration involves walking outdoors.

Public transportation in Carthage is efficient and affordable, and taxis are available throughout the area. If you prefer a more guided experience, there are local tours that offer a comprehensive exploration of the Carthaginian ruins, often including transportation from Tunis or Sidi Bou Said. Many of these tours are led by knowledgeable guides who can provide in-depth information about the historical significance of the sites and bring the ancient city to life.

Carthage is an essential destination for anyone visiting Tunisia, offering a fascinating glimpse into the past and a wealth of historical landmarks to explore. From the ancient ruins of Byrsa Hill and the Antonine Baths to the harbors and the Tophet, each site in Carthage provides a unique insight into the city's past as a dominant power in the Mediterranean world. Whether you are a history lover, an archaeology enthusiast, or simply someone interested in experiencing one of the most important ancient cities of antiquity, a visit to Carthage is sure to be a memorable and enriching experience.

Blue & White Village of Sidi Bou Said

Sidi Bou Said is one of the most picturesque and enchanting villages in Tunisia, offering a mesmerizing blend of stunning architecture, tranquil Mediterranean views, and a rich cultural history. Famous for its signature whitewashed buildings adorned with blue shutters, doors, and wrought-iron balconies, Sidi Bou Said exudes an atmosphere of calm and beauty that has drawn artists, writers, and travelers from around the world. Situated on a hilltop overlooking the Mediterranean Sea, the village is just a short distance from Tunis and Carthage, making it an ideal day-trip destination for those wanting to experience the charm of Tunisia's coastal landscape combined with a rich history.

To get to Sidi Bou Said, visitors can easily take a taxi from Tunis, which takes about 20 minutes, depending on traffic. Alternatively, you can use the **Tunis Light Rail**, which is a quick and convenient way to travel from the center of Tunis to Sidi Bou Said. The **TGM (Tunis-Goulette-Marsa)** suburban train line connects Tunis to the coastal towns, and **Sidi Bou Said** is one of its main stops. The journey from Tunis's central train station to Sidi Bou Said takes roughly 30 minutes, and trains run frequently throughout the day. This mode of transportation is popular with both locals and tourists, offering a scenic ride along the coastline, passing through neighborhoods such as La Marsa and the vibrant port area of **La Goulette** before reaching the hilltop village.

Upon arrival in Sidi Bou Said, you'll immediately be struck by the stunning white and blue color scheme that covers the village. The traditional architecture of Sidi Bou Said reflects a blend of **Arabic**, **Ottoman**, and **French** influences, which is evident in the intricate designs of the houses, streets, and public spaces. The blue shutters and doors are an iconic feature of the village, and they are often associated with the Mediterranean region, where the colors were thought to symbolize peace and protect against the harshness of the sun. As you walk through the village's narrow cobblestone streets, you'll encounter a series of charming whitewashed buildings, vibrant bougainvillea, and intricate tilework that contribute to the village's unique atmosphere. Sidi Bou Said is often described as a place where time seems to stand still, allowing visitors to step back and experience a timeless corner of Tunisia.

One of the main attractions in Sidi Bou Said is the **Café des Nattes**, a historic café that sits at the heart of the village and is a popular spot for both locals and tourists. The café, with its traditional blue and white decor, has been a favorite gathering place for artists and intellectuals for many years, including famous figures such as Paul Klee and the philosopher **Albert Camus**, who once visited the village regularly. Today, the café remains a symbol of Sidi Bou Said's artistic heritage, offering visitors a chance to relax with a cup of mint tea or coffee while enjoying the stunning views of the sea and surrounding hills. There is no entry fee to visit the café, but it's customary to order something if you plan to sit for a while, and the café typically operates from morning until late afternoon, though hours may vary.

The main street in Sidi Bou Said, known as **Rue Hedi Zarrouk**, is a popular spot for leisurely strolls. Lined with cafés, art galleries, and boutique shops, this street provides a wonderful opportunity to experience the laid-back, bohemian atmosphere of the village. The street leads toward the **Place Sidi Bou Said**, a small but charming square where visitors can stop to take in the view or browse local shops selling crafts, jewelry, and souvenirs. The village is a hub for Tunisian craftsmanship, and it's an excellent place to purchase traditional **handmade pottery**, **textiles**, and **metalwork**. While you won't find massive shopping malls here, the small artisan shops add to the village's charm and authenticity. One particularly notable item to look for is the **blue-and-white pottery**, often featuring intricate patterns and geometric designs that reflect the region's traditional craftsmanship.

Another key attraction in Sidi Bou Said is the **Ennejma Ezzahra Palace**, a grand historic building that is one of the most important landmarks in the village. The palace was built in the early 20th century by the wealthy aristocrat **Roushdi Pasha**, a member of Tunisia's ruling class under the French protectorate. The palace is a beautiful example of neo-Moorish architecture, and it's renowned for its stunning gardens and intricate tilework. The palace houses the **Centre des Musiques Arabes et Méditerranéennes** (Center for Arab and Mediterranean Music), and it is often used for concerts, cultural events, and exhibitions. Visitors can explore the palace's stunning interiors, including its large, intricately decorated rooms, as well as its peaceful courtyards and gardens, which offer a glimpse into the grandeur of Tunisia's aristocratic past. The palace is open to the public daily, with regular visiting hours from 9 AM to 5 PM. The entry fee is around 8-10 TND, depending on whether you wish to attend a concert or cultural event.

Sidi Bou Said is also a great place for hiking and enjoying the natural beauty of the surrounding area. The village is perched on a hill, providing excellent views over the Mediterranean and the nearby coastline. Visitors can take a stroll to the nearby **Carthage National Park**, a large natural area where you can enjoy the lush vegetation and panoramic views of the Gulf of Tunis. The park is a serene place to relax, take photos, or enjoy a peaceful walk along its well-maintained trails. It's also worth mentioning the nearby **La Marsa** beach, which is only a short drive away, where visitors can unwind by the sea, swim, or simply enjoy the coastline.

For those interested in art and culture, Sidi Bou Said offers a number of small **art galleries** that showcase the work of local artists. Many of the galleries focus on contemporary Tunisian art, ranging from paintings to sculptures and ceramics. The village's artistic community is deeply connected to the history and identity of Sidi Bou Said, and several exhibitions are held throughout the year, featuring emerging artists as well as established names in the Tunisian art world. Some galleries also sell artworks, so it's a great place to pick up a unique piece of Tunisian art as a memento of your visit.

Sidi Bou Said is also well known for its lively atmosphere during the evening hours. As the sun sets over the Mediterranean, the village comes alive with locals and tourists alike enjoying the cool evening breeze. Many of the village's cafés and restaurants offer outdoor seating, and you'll find that dining in Sidi Bou Said provides a beautiful combination of great food and scenic views. **Seafood** is a highlight of the local cuisine, and several restaurants along the waterfront serve freshly caught fish and other Mediterranean specialties. Visitors can enjoy a leisurely dinner while watching the sun set over the horizon, creating a memorable dining experience.

While Sidi Bou Said is one of the most visited destinations in Tunisia, it remains a peaceful retreat where visitors can enjoy a slower pace of life, taking in the beauty of the village and its surroundings. Whether you are interested in history, architecture, art, or simply want to relax in a stunning setting, Sidi Bou Said offers something for everyone. The charm of the village lies in its simplicity: its cobbled streets, whitewashed buildings, vibrant blue accents, and spectacular views create an idyllic and timeless atmosphere. It's a place that invites you to wander, explore, and lose yourself in its tranquil beauty.

Sidi Bou Said is a must-visit destination for anyone traveling to Tunisia, offering a perfect blend of natural beauty, cultural heritage, and artistic charm. Its white-and-blue streets, picturesque views, historic buildings, and vibrant arts scene make it one of the most beautiful and memorable places in the country. Whether you are looking for a place to relax, explore, or immerse yourself in Tunisia's rich history and culture, Sidi Bou Said is the ideal destination.

Exploring Sahara Desert

The Sahara Desert, the largest hot desert on Earth, spans over several countries in North Africa, and Tunisia offers a unique gateway to its mesmerizing landscapes. Tunisia's portion of the Sahara is a place of unearthly beauty and an ideal destination for travelers looking for adventure, solitude, and cultural exploration. The vast sea of dunes, the quiet stillness, and the breathtaking starry nights combine to create a destination that is unlike any other. This piece of the Sahara is home to tranquil oases, small villages, and unique desert experiences, making it one of Tunisia's most intriguing destinations.

Reaching the Sahara Desert in Tunisia usually involves traveling to **Tozeur**, a town located approximately 500 kilometers south of Tunis. Tozeur serves as the main hub for desert exploration and provides easy access to the surrounding desert areas. From Tunis, visitors can travel by car, bus, or train, though the journey by train offers a scenic route through the countryside and takes around 7-8 hours. Alternatively, flights are available from Tunis to **Tozeur-**

Nefta Airport, making it the quickest option for those on a tighter schedule. Upon arrival in Tozeur, travelers can easily find a range of accommodation options, from budget hotels to more luxurious resorts, and start their desert adventure.

Once in Tozeur, the Sahara experience begins with camel treks, the quintessential desert activity. The camels, known as the "ships of the desert," offer travelers a slow-paced, authentic way to experience the vast dunes. Camel treks in the Sahara typically last anywhere from a few hours to several days, depending on the level of adventure desired. For shorter excursions, you can opt for a half-day trek that takes you into the surrounding dunes and offers stunning views of the desert's undulating landscape. Longer treks, which last for one or more nights, provide the opportunity to venture deeper into the desert, sometimes as far as the famous **Chott el Jerid**, a massive salt flat that stretches for miles. These extended trips offer a more immersive experience, with travelers staying overnight in traditional Berber-style desert camps, where they can enjoy warm meals under the stars and sleep in comfortable tents.

Prices for camel treks can vary widely depending on the duration and the level of comfort you want. Short treks usually start around **30-40 TND (around $10-15 USD)** for a half-day ride. For longer treks, you might expect to pay around **100-150 TND (approximately $35-50 USD)** for a full-day trek, and multi-day trips can cost anywhere from **250-500 TND (around $80-160 USD)** per person, including accommodation and meals at desert camps. Many camel trek operators offer all-inclusive packages, which cover transport from Tozeur to the desert, guides, food, and overnight stays in the desert. Prices may vary depending on the time of year, with the peak season being from October to April, when the weather is more moderate and conducive to desert travel.

In addition to camel treks, there are other activities for those looking to explore the Sahara in different ways. **4x4 excursions** are popular for travelers who wish to cover more ground and explore the desert's rugged terrain. These off-road tours often take visitors across sand dunes, through ancient villages, and to remote desert locations that are inaccessible by camel. These excursions can be tailored to your interests and can include visits to filming locations from *Star Wars*, including the famous **Matmata troglodyte dwellings** and the **Ksar Ouled Soltane**, a Berber village with distinctive mud-brick architecture. A 4x4 tour of the desert typically costs **80-150 TND (around $25-50 USD)** for a half-day adventure, with full-day tours costing more.

For those interested in the desert's natural beauty, visiting the **oasis towns** is a must. Tozeur itself is famous for its lush palm groves and its proximity to the **Chott el Jerid** salt flats, which make for an otherworldly landscape. The salt flats, shimmering under the sun, seem to stretch to infinity, creating a surreal setting that is particularly stunning at sunrise or sunset. Visitors can explore the salt flats on camelback or by 4x4, and the views of the horizon are unforgettable. Just a short drive from Tozeur is the **Tamerza Oasis**, a beautiful hidden gem with waterfalls cascading through a palm-fringed valley, offering a stark contrast to the arid landscape that surrounds it. The **Mides**

Gorge, another nearby attraction, offers dramatic canyon views and provides opportunities for light trekking.

In addition to the natural beauty, the Sahara Desert in Tunisia is deeply connected to its **cultural heritage**. The **Berber** people, who have lived in the desert for thousands of years, are a fundamental part of the experience. Many desert excursions are led by Berber guides who not only know the landscape but also share their rich traditions, history, and survival techniques in the harsh desert environment. Visitors may have the opportunity to visit traditional Berber villages, where they can interact with local families, sample traditional food, and learn about the unique way of life in the desert. A visit to a traditional Berber home, built in the earth, offers a fascinating insight into how the people of the desert have adapted to such a challenging environment.

One of the highlights of any visit to the Sahara Desert is the **night sky**. With its complete absence of light pollution, the desert offers unparalleled stargazing opportunities. Visitors who venture into the desert for multi-day camel treks or 4x4 tours will be treated to one of the most mesmerizing skies on Earth. The Sahara's clear skies allow you to see the Milky Way in all its glory, as well as countless constellations and celestial bodies. Desert camps typically set up their tents in the open, providing a comfortable place to sleep under the stars. Spending the night in the Sahara, away from the noise and distractions of city life, is an almost spiritual experience, offering a deep sense of peace and connection to nature. Campfires are often lit in the evening, and visitors can enjoy a meal of traditional

couscous or **tagine** while listening to local **Berber music**, which adds to the magic of the experience.

While the Sahara Desert is known for its vastness and stark beauty, it also offers a unique blend of **adventure**, **history**, and **cultural richness**. Travelers are not only drawn to the physical aspects of the desert but also to the feeling of stepping into a place that is timeless, remote, and rich with stories. The desert's remote oases, historical sites, and interaction with the Berber people provide a deeper understanding of Tunisia's past and its relationship with the Sahara.

To make the most of your trip to the Sahara Desert, it's essential to come prepared. **Comfortable clothing** is crucial, especially for camel treks. Light, breathable clothes, a hat, sunglasses, and sturdy shoes are recommended for daytime activities, while a jacket or sweater may be necessary for cooler desert nights. Travelers should also ensure they have **plenty of water** and **sunscreen** to stay hydrated and protected from the sun.

Visiting the Sahara Desert is an unforgettable experience that allows you to immerse yourself in one of the most unique environments on Earth. Whether you're trekking on camelback, exploring ancient oases, or gazing up at the brilliant night sky, the Sahara Desert in Tunisia offers a sense of adventure, serenity, and wonder that stays with you long after you've left its golden sands behind.

Coastal Gems: Hammamet, Monastir & Djerba Island

Tunisia's coastline, stretching along the Mediterranean Sea, is one of the country's most alluring features, offering sun-soaked beaches, charming towns, and a rich blend of history, culture, and modern leisure. Among the most celebrated coastal gems in Tunisia are **Hammamet**, **Monastir**, and **Djerba Island**—each of which offers its own unique appeal, from tranquil resorts to historic landmarks, all set against a stunning Mediterranean backdrop. Whether you are seeking relaxation on golden sands, exploration of ancient fortresses, or immersion in local traditions, these destinations are essential stops for any visitor to Tunisia.

Hammamet, located just 60 kilometers southeast of Tunis, is one of Tunisia's most popular beach resorts, known for its beautiful beaches, crystal-clear waters, and vibrant tourism scene. The town's charm lies in its blend of modern hotels and charming old town streets, where narrow alleys lined with whitewashed houses meet the lively promenade. The **medina** (old town) is the heart of Hammamet, where you can explore traditional markets, visit the historic **Kasbah** (fortress), and wander through streets filled with craft shops selling jewelry, carpets, and leather goods. The **Kasbah**, perched on a hill, offers fantastic views of the town and the Mediterranean Sea, making it a must-see for visitors. The town is also home to beautiful **gardens**, such as the **Bel Azur Garden**, where you can stroll among fragrant flowers and enjoy the lush greenery that contrasts with the arid landscapes found in other parts of the country.

Hammamet is also famous for its extensive stretches of sandy beaches, which are some of the best in Tunisia. The beaches here cater to a variety of tastes, from quieter, more private spots perfect for relaxation to bustling stretches filled with water sports activities such as **jet skiing**, **windsurfing**, and **parasailing**. Visitors can also take boat trips from the coast to explore nearby coves and enjoy the beautiful Mediterranean waters. For a more cultural experience, **Carthage Land** amusement park, a family-friendly destination, offers fun for all ages with water slides, roller coasters, and themed attractions related to Tunisia's rich history.

The town is well-connected to the rest of Tunisia, and reaching it from **Tunis** is straightforward by train, bus, or private car. The drive takes about an hour, and taxis are readily available. Hammamet is also home to a range of accommodations, from budget-friendly hotels to luxurious resorts with all-inclusive packages, making it a versatile destination for various types of travelers. Rental costs for activities vary, but beach chair rentals typically cost around **10-15 TND (about $3-5 USD)** for the day, while water sports such as jet skiing might range from **50-100 TND ($15-35 USD)** per hour.

Further down the coast is **Monastir**, a town steeped in history and natural beauty. Located about 150 kilometers south of Tunis, Monastir is easily accessible by car, train, or bus. The town's old center is home to one of Tunisia's most iconic landmarks: the **Ribat of Monastir**. This ancient fortress, dating back to the 8th century, was built by the Arabs to defend the coast against pirate raids. Today, the Ribat is a fascinating museum where visitors can learn about Tunisia's early Islamic history while exploring its impressive towers, courtyards, and view over the sea. Another important landmark is the **Bourguiba Mausoleum**, which honors **Habib Bourguiba**, the first president of Tunisia. Located in the heart of Monastir, this mausoleum is surrounded by a beautiful garden and provides visitors with a glimpse into the political history of modern Tunisia. The **Ribat** and **Mausoleum** are both open to visitors, with minimal entry fees around **5-10 TND ($2-3 USD)**.

Monastir is also known for its beautiful coastline, which is lined with sandy beaches and luxurious resorts. The town has been a popular tourist destination for years, offering a wide range of accommodations, from charming boutique hotels to all-inclusive luxury resorts. Visitors to Monastir can indulge in the usual beachside activities, such as swimming, sunbathing, and water sports, but the area also offers opportunities to explore the **Moknine**, a town known for its pottery workshops, and **Sousse**, a nearby city that is home to Tunisia's largest marina and a UNESCO-listed medina.

Monastir's proximity to **Sousse** and **Port El Kantaoui**, another famous resort area, allows for easy day trips to explore Tunisia's other coastal gems. The town is also a great base for exploring the wider **Sahel** region, with its picturesque villages, olive groves, and historical sites. Transportation to Monastir from Tunis can be done by train or private car, with journeys taking roughly two hours. As for activity costs, most beach clubs and water sports in Monastir charge similar rates to those in Hammamet, with **jet ski rentals** averaging around **50-80 TND ($17-27 USD)** per hour.

The third coastal jewel of Tunisia is **Djerba Island**, located off the southern coast of Tunisia, accessible by a bridge that connects the island to the mainland at **Ajim**. Known for its relaxed atmosphere, pristine beaches, and rich cultural heritage, Djerba is often referred to as the "Island of Dreams." To reach Djerba, visitors can fly into **Djerba-Zarzis International Airport** from Tunis or other major cities, or they can take a bus or taxi from **Gabes**, a nearby coastal town on the mainland. Alternatively, those traveling from **Hammamet** or **Monastir** can take a longer but scenic journey by car or bus, which takes around four to five hours.

Djerba is a place where relaxation meets exploration. The island's beaches are its main draw, with crystal-clear waters and soft, golden sand that stretches as far as the eye can see. Visitors can enjoy a range of activities, including **snorkeling**, **kite surfing**, and **fishing**. The island also boasts several well-preserved historical sites, such as the **El Ghriba Synagogue**, which is one of the oldest Jewish synagogues in the world. El Ghriba is a major pilgrimage site for Jews, and its striking architecture and serene atmosphere make it a must-visit for those interested in Tunisia's religious history. The nearby **Houmt Souk**, the island's capital, is known for its bustling souks (markets), where visitors can purchase **handmade pottery**, **leather goods**, and **silver jewelry**.

Djerba is also known for its traditional **villages** where the old way of life is still maintained. The **Henchir El Hara** village, for example, offers visitors a glimpse into the traditional architecture and culture of the island's rural inhabitants. The island is also home to **beautiful resorts**, many of which offer beachfront access and provide a range of activities for guests, including **spa treatments**, **horseback riding**, and **cultural excursions**.

For visitors looking for adventure, Djerba offers the chance to explore its diverse landscapes, including **palm groves**, **fishing villages**, and **salt flats**, which offer stunning backdrops for photography. One of the island's unique features is the **Djerba Explore Park**, where visitors can see a crocodile farm and explore the island's natural habitat. Visitors can rent bicycles or ATVs to explore the island on their own, with rentals typically costing around **20-30 TND ($7-10 USD)** per day. A visit to the island's famous **marketplace** is also an experience in itself, with bargaining being a cherished part of the island's culture.

Hammamet, Monastir, and Djerba Island each offer distinct and unforgettable coastal experiences in Tunisia. Whether you're looking to relax on beautiful beaches, immerse yourself in history and culture, or enjoy the outdoor activities available along the Mediterranean, these coastal gems provide a diverse range of experiences that will captivate any traveler. With accessible transport, affordable activities, and a wide range of accommodation options,

Tunisia's coastline is an ideal destination for those seeking both adventure and relaxation.

Roman Ruins of Dougga & El Djem

The Roman ruins of **Dougga** and **El Djem** stand as two of Tunisia's most remarkable and well-preserved archaeological sites, offering visitors a fascinating glimpse into the grandeur of Roman civilization in North Africa. Both sites are significant not only for their architectural splendor but also for their historical and cultural importance, showcasing the influence of Rome in this part of the ancient world.

Located approximately **100 kilometers southwest of Tunis**, the ancient city of **Dougga** is a UNESCO World Heritage site and often considered one of the best-preserved Roman archaeological sites in Tunisia. To reach Dougga, visitors typically travel by car or taxi from Tunis, which takes around 1.5 to 2 hours. While there are also buses that operate from Tunis to the nearby town of **Testour**, it is usually easier to rent a car or take a private taxi to reach the site directly, as public transportation options are limited and may require additional travel to the village before reaching the ruins.

Dougga, which was once known as *Thugga*, was an important Roman town that flourished during the empire's peak. Its ruins are scattered across a hilltop, providing a dramatic view of the surrounding countryside. The site is renowned for its well-preserved **theater**, **temples**, **baths**, and **civic buildings**, with much of its structure still intact. Visitors can explore the **Capitolium**, an ancient temple dedicated to the Roman gods, which stands proudly at the highest point of the site. This temple, though somewhat weathered, still conveys the grandeur of Roman religious architecture. Adjacent to it is the **Roman theater**, which is still used for occasional performances, though its seats and stage are in remarkable condition, and its acoustics are impressive for a structure built nearly two millennia ago. The theater, with a capacity of around 3,500 spectators, is one of the finest examples of Roman engineering in Tunisia. The **ancient baths** of Dougga, with their remnants of vaulted ceilings and intricate mosaics, offer an insight into the daily life of the Roman elite. The **Roman villas** with intricate mosaic floors and residential areas provide a glimpse of domestic life during the height of the empire.

Among the most significant aspects of Dougga are the **Tomb of the Male Child** and the **Temple of Juno Caelestis**, both of which have become iconic symbols of the site. The **Temple of Juno Caelestis**, dedicated to the Carthaginian goddess Tanit, is particularly significant as it highlights the blend of Roman and local Carthaginian culture that defined the region. The mosaics found here are intricate and colorful, showcasing scenes from Roman mythology and daily life.

The ruins of Dougga are open to the public, and the site has well-maintained paths that guide visitors through the various structures. Visitors can easily spend a few hours exploring the site, but those interested in in-depth exploration and history should allocate half a day to take in the full scope of the ruins. **Entry fees** for Dougga are typically **12-15 TND (about $4-5 USD)**, with **student discounts** available. It is advisable to arrive early in the day to avoid the heat, especially during the summer months, as the site offers little shade. There are also **local guides** available on-site for an additional fee, often around **20-30 TND** ($7-10 USD), which can greatly enhance the experience by providing detailed explanations of the history and significance of the ruins.

El Djem, located about **200 kilometers south of Tunis**, is another UNESCO World Heritage site and perhaps one of the most spectacular remnants of Roman architecture in Africa. The most famous feature of El Djem is the **Colosseum**, a magnificent amphitheater that rivals its Roman counterparts in size and preservation. El Djem's amphitheater, one of the largest ever built by the Romans, was capable of seating **35,000 spectators**, and it is often referred to as the "African Colosseum." It is remarkable not only for its size but also for its state of preservation. Standing on the outer rim of the arena, visitors can look down into the sandy floor where gladiators once fought, and the tiered seating offers an impressive view of the structure's architectural genius.

The **El Djem amphitheater**, constructed in the early 3rd century AD, is an awe-inspiring example of Roman engineering, with its arches and massive stone walls still intact. Unlike its counterpart in Rome, El Djem's amphitheater is less crowded and offers a more intimate experience. Visitors can walk around the arena, explore the underground chambers that were once used to house gladiators and animals, and climb to the upper levels for stunning views over the surrounding town and countryside. The site's remarkable preservation allows visitors to get a sense of what it must have been like to witness ancient Roman games, offering both an educational and immersive experience.

In addition to the amphitheater, the **El Djem Archaeological Museum**, located adjacent to the site, houses an impressive collection of mosaics, statues, and artifacts excavated from the ruins. These objects provide further insight into the daily lives of the people who once inhabited the city. Some of the mosaics on display are incredibly intricate, depicting scenes of mythology, battle, and daily Roman life. The museum's collection offers a deeper understanding of the region's rich Roman history and its cultural integration into the wider empire.

Getting to El Djem from Tunis is relatively straightforward. Visitors can take a **train** from Tunis to **El Djem**, which takes around **3-4 hours** and offers a scenic journey through Tunisia's rural landscape. Alternatively, travelers can rent a car, which takes about 2.5 to 3 hours, or take a **taxi** or **bus**. Upon arrival, the amphitheater is easily accessible, and most visitors head directly to the main site. **Entry fees** to the amphitheater are typically around **10-12 TND (about $3-4 USD)**, with discounts for students. The museum has a separate entry fee, usually around **5 TND (about $1.50 USD)**, and is a great complement to the amphitheater visit. Most of the site is open-air, so it is best to visit early in the morning or later in the afternoon, especially during the hot summer months, to avoid the midday heat.

Both Dougga and El Djem are accessible year-round, but visitors should be mindful of the heat during the summer, particularly at Dougga, where little shade exists. While the ruins can be explored independently, hiring a local guide can enrich the experience, offering not only historical context but also personal anecdotes that help bring the ancient world to life. Many guides are available at the entrance to both sites, and it is recommended to negotiate a price in advance or opt for official guides that are licensed by the government.

The **Roman ruins of Dougga and El Djem** offer a profound and captivating journey into Tunisia's rich Roman heritage. From the sprawling ruins at Dougga, with its temples, theaters, and villas, to the dramatic amphitheater at El Djem, these sites provide a striking reminder of the architectural ingenuity and cultural influence of Rome. Whether you are a history enthusiast, an architecture lover, or simply someone who appreciates ancient ruins, these two sites offer an unforgettable experience. Combining these destinations with Tunisia's vibrant culture and natural beauty makes for an enriching and well-rounded visit to the country, allowing you to step back in time and witness the magnificence of the Roman Empire in one of its farthest-reaching provinces.

Atlas Mountains & Kairouan

The **Atlas Mountains** and **Kairouan** are two of Tunisia's most captivating regions, offering visitors a chance to immerse themselves in both natural beauty and the profound history of this North African country. From the majestic peaks of the Atlas Mountains, where adventure, hiking, and stunning views await, to the spiritual and cultural heart of Tunisia in the ancient city of Kairouan, these destinations provide diverse experiences that appeal to nature lovers, history buffs, and anyone seeking to understand Tunisia's rich cultural heritage.

The **Atlas Mountains**, which stretch across Tunisia's western border, form a natural barrier between the Mediterranean coast and the desert regions of the south. The range includes a variety of dramatic landscapes, from rugged peaks and deep valleys to lush oases and dense forests. The mountains are not only home to diverse flora and fauna but also rich in Berber culture, with small, traditional villages scattered throughout the region, offering a glimpse into a way of life that has remained largely unchanged for centuries. The Atlas Mountains in Tunisia are an excellent destination for **hiking**, **trekking**, and **nature exploration**, with many well-marked trails that wind through forests, past ancient ruins, and up to breathtaking viewpoints overlooking the surrounding landscapes. The mountains are easily accessible from **Tunis**, and the nearest towns, such as **Ain Draham** and **Tabarka**, serve as convenient bases for those looking to explore the region. From **Tunis**, it is roughly a 2-hour drive to Ain Draham, a town that sits at the foot of the Atlas

Mountains and is known for its cool climate, lush vegetation, and vibrant Berber heritage. Tabarka, further to the north, is also a great entry point into the Atlas region and offers access to both the mountains and the beautiful coastline. From these towns, visitors can arrange guided treks or explore on their own, taking in the picturesque landscapes of **oak and pine forests**, tranquil valleys, and sparkling rivers. The Atlas Mountains are a haven for nature enthusiasts, offering a chance to connect with the region's unique ecosystem, including native species such as the **Barbary sheep**, **wild boar**, and a variety of bird species, including the **Eagle Owl**.

For those interested in **cultural experiences**, the Atlas region also provides opportunities to visit traditional Berber villages. Many of these villages have retained their ancient customs and architecture, with houses built in traditional styles, such as the **stone and clay dwellings** that blend seamlessly into the natural landscape. Some villages, like **Tamerza** in the south of the mountains, are known for their beautiful palm groves and **oasis**, making them the perfect place to explore the intersection of nature and culture. Visitors can take part in **local handicraft workshops**, where artisans demonstrate the time-honored skills of **weaving**, **pottery making**, and **jewelry crafting**, and learn about the unique **Berber language** and customs that continue to thrive in these isolated communities. The Atlas Mountains are also home to several important historical sites, including the **Roman ruins of Dougga** to the southeast and the ancient city of **Carthage**, which offer a fascinating contrast to the natural beauty of the region. Trekking through these mountains provides a chance to see both the natural landscape and the remnants of Tunisia's complex and diverse history.

For those seeking more structured activities, there are a variety of **tour operators** offering guided tours that include **hiking** and **cultural excursions** into the mountains. The cost for a guided day trip typically ranges from **50-100 TND ($15-30 USD)** per person, depending on the level of service and length of the tour. Visitors can also find **rental services** for outdoor equipment such as **hiking boots**, **walking sticks**, and **climbing gear**, which typically cost around **20-50 TND ($7-17 USD)** per day. The best time to visit the Atlas Mountains is during the spring (March to May) and autumn (September to November) months when the weather is cooler and the landscape is lush and green. In the summer, the mountains can get quite hot, especially at lower elevations, while the winter months bring snow to the higher peaks, providing opportunities for those interested in experiencing a snowy landscape or taking part in **winter sports**.

Just a few hours drive south of the Atlas Mountains is **Kairouan**, one of Tunisia's most significant historical and religious cities. Founded in the 7th century, Kairouan is regarded as the fourth holiest city in Islam, after **Mecca**, **Medina**, and **Jerusalem**. The city's significance as a center of Islamic scholarship and spirituality is unmatched, and it has long been a destination for Muslim pilgrims. It is also known for its well-preserved **Islamic architecture**, which has earned it a place on the UNESCO World Heritage list.

To get to Kairouan, visitors can easily travel from **Tunis** by train, bus, or private car. The city is located about **160**

kilometers south of Tunis, and the journey by car typically takes around 2.5 hours. Kairouan's location in central Tunisia makes it an accessible and convenient stop for travelers heading to other destinations, such as the **Sahara Desert** or the coastal city of **Sousse**. Upon arrival, visitors are immediately drawn to the imposing **Great Mosque of Kairouan**, also known as the **Mosque of Uqba**. Built in the 9th century, this mosque is considered one of the finest examples of Islamic architecture in North Africa. Its vast courtyard, surrounded by graceful arcades, and its massive prayer hall with intricately decorated arches and columns, create an atmosphere of awe and reverence. The mosque is open to visitors, though non-Muslim visitors may not be allowed to enter the inner prayer hall. It is recommended to check in advance and dress modestly when visiting.

Another must-see in Kairouan is the **Aghlabid Basins**, a series of ancient water reservoirs that were built by the Aghlabid dynasty in the 9th century to supply the city with water. The **Basins of the Aghlabids** are impressive in their scale and engineering, and visitors can walk around the large water basins, which were once used to store water that was distributed throughout the city. The **Zaouia of Sidi Sahab**, a small mosque and tomb complex, is another highlight of the city. This peaceful site is home to the tomb of the companion of the Prophet Muhammad, **Sidi Sahab**, and is known for its beautiful **mosaic decorations** and tranquil atmosphere. The **medina** (old city) of Kairouan is a labyrinth of narrow streets lined with whitewashed houses, local markets, and artisan shops where visitors can purchase **traditional textiles**, **ceramics**, and **handmade** carpets. The **Kairouan souks** are an excellent place to experience the local culture and try traditional **Tunisian sweets**, such as **makroud**, a semolina cake filled with dates and nuts.

Entry fees to the major attractions in Kairouan are generally affordable, with **entry to the Great Mosque** costing around **5 TND (approximately $2 USD)** for non-Muslim visitors, and other sites like the **Aghlabid Basins** and **Zaouia of Sidi Sahab** charging around **3-5 TND ($1-2 USD)**. Visitors should take note that Kairouan is an important religious city, so modest dress is required, particularly when visiting mosques and other sacred sites.

Kairouan's **rich history**, **Islamic architecture**, and **spiritual significance** make it an essential stop for anyone interested in understanding the roots of Tunisia's cultural and religious heritage. It offers a peaceful, reflective atmosphere that contrasts with the bustling cities along the coast, providing a deep dive into Tunisia's Islamic past.

The combination of the **Atlas Mountains** and **Kairouan** presents visitors with the opportunity to explore both the natural beauty and historical depth of Tunisia. Whether hiking through the rugged peaks of the Atlas Mountains, experiencing the quiet charm of Berber villages, or stepping back in time in the sacred streets of Kairouan, these regions offer a unique and rewarding experience for all types of travelers. The ease of access, affordable prices, and remarkable attractions make these destinations an essential part of any Tunisian itinerary.

Tozeur & the Chott El Jerid Salt Flats

Tozeur and the nearby **Chott El Jerid Salt Flats** form one of Tunisia's most iconic and mesmerizing regions, offering an experience that blends natural beauty, adventure, and an immersion into the vast, otherworldly landscapes of the desert. Situated in the southwestern part of Tunisia, Tozeur serves as a gateway to the **Sahara Desert** and is known for its dramatic scenery, historic architecture, and its role as a hub for desert tourism.

Tozeur is located about **500 kilometers south of Tunis**, and can be accessed by road or air. The most common way to get to Tozeur is by flying into **Tozeur-Nefta International Airport**, which is located just a short distance from the town center. The airport services both domestic and international flights, with regular connections to **Tunis** and other major cities in Tunisia. Alternatively, visitors can travel by **bus** or **train** from Tunis to Tozeur, which takes approximately **7-8 hours by bus** or **6 hours by train**. Many tourists opt to rent a car for more flexibility in exploring the region, as Tozeur is also a starting point for desert excursions to the nearby **Chott El Jerid** salt flats, **Tamerza**, and other desert oases.

Upon arrival in Tozeur, the town itself offers a variety of attractions. The **medina** of Tozeur is a delightful labyrinth of narrow streets lined with **traditional houses**, many made from **date palm wood**, which is a defining characteristic of the area. The architecture is unique, with intricate patterns on the facades of buildings created using palm fronds. The town is often referred to as the **"oasis of palm trees"** because of its dense palm groves, which cover much of the landscape and provide a cool respite from the surrounding desert heat. The **Tozeur Oasis** is one of the largest in Tunisia, with over **400,000 palm trees** that have sustained the local population for centuries. Walking through the oasis, visitors can enjoy the tranquil atmosphere and explore the many small gardens, fruit groves, and ponds that dot the landscape.

One of the most striking features of Tozeur is the **Dar Chrait Museum**, housed in a traditional palm-frond building, which offers an insight into the region's history, culture, and desert life. The museum features a collection of **artifacts**, including old tools, pottery, traditional clothing, and the famous **Chott El Jerid** salt flats photography, highlighting the relationship between the people and the desert. The **Zenata Souk**, located in the heart of the town, is another must-visit spot for travelers. It is a bustling market where visitors can shop for local goods such as **handmade carpets**, **woven baskets**, **ceramics**, and **dates**. The market also sells **traditional Tunisian jewelry** and **spices**, offering a taste of the local culture.

While Tozeur itself is a captivating town, its main attraction lies in its proximity to the **Chott El Jerid**, a vast and surreal salt flat that stretches for over **5,000 square kilometers**. The Chott El Jerid is one of the largest **salt deserts** in the world, and its otherworldly appearance makes it a must-see destination for adventurers and photographers. The salt flats are located about **20 kilometers east of Tozeur**, and they are easily accessible by car or through organized tours. The Chott El Jerid is especially famous for its dramatic **sunset views**, when the setting sun casts a golden glow across the salt crusts, creating an almost ethereal, shimmering effect on the flat terrain. The salt flats are often compared to a frozen sea, with vast expanses of cracked earth creating a stark, yet captivating landscape.

Visitors to the Chott El Jerid can take part in a variety of **desert excursions**, which can be arranged from Tozeur. These excursions typically involve traveling in **4x4 vehicles**, which can easily navigate the rough terrain. Many tour operators offer guided trips into the desert, with prices usually ranging from **60-150 TND ($20-50 USD)** for a half-day trip. These tours typically include stops at key points of interest, such as the **Hassi R'Mel**, a traditional Berber village, or the **Tamerza Canyon**, a stunning oasis town that is also within driving distance of Tozeur. Some tours even include the option of **camel rides** into the salt flats or **overnight stays** at desert camps, where guests can experience the desert in its full glory, enjoy a traditional **Tunisian dinner**, and stargaze under the clear, pollution-free skies.

The **Chott El Jerid** is particularly famous for being featured in numerous **film productions**, including the **Star Wars** series, which used the vast desert as a filming location for scenes on the fictional planet of **Tatooine**. Fans of the movies will recognize some of the landscape from the iconic scenes set in the desert. Visitors can also find remnants of **Star Wars sets**, such as the **Tatooine house** in the town of **Matmata**, not far from Tozeur. Tours to these locations can be organized as part of the desert excursions from Tozeur.

When visiting the **Chott El Jerid**, the best time to go is during the **spring (March to May)** or **autumn (September to November)** months, when the weather is more moderate. In the summer months, the temperatures can soar above **40°C (104°F)**, making it challenging to explore without adequate preparation. Visitors should wear light, breathable clothing, and ensure they have plenty of **water** and **sunscreen**. It is also advisable to bring a **hat** and **sunglasses** to protect against the harsh sun, especially when venturing into the salt flats.

Although the salt flats are generally free to explore, there are some **entrance fees** for certain areas or **guides**. The price for a **4x4 desert excursion** typically includes the guide and vehicle, with **fees ranging from 30-70 TND ($10-25 USD)** for a short, half-day excursion, while full-day tours may cost upwards of **100 TND ($30 USD)**. **Camel rides** are an additional cost, usually priced at around **20-30 TND ($7-10 USD)** for an hour-long ride. **Overnight stays** in desert camps are also available, with prices typically ranging from **100-150 TND ($30-50 USD)** per person, including meals and entertainment.

The **Chott El Jerid Salt Flats** are truly a unique experience for any traveler, offering a surreal, alien landscape that is a stark contrast to the bustling towns along the coast. The sense of isolation and beauty that permeates this region is awe-inspiring, and for those willing to venture into the desert, it offers some of the most unforgettable views in Tunisia.

Tozeur and the **Chott El Jerid** are essential destinations for any traveler looking to explore the depths of Tunisia's natural beauty and rich cultural heritage. Whether it's the tranquil oasis of Tozeur, with its palm-lined streets and Berber villages, or the vast, ethereal landscapes of the salt flats, this region offers a range of experiences that cater to all types of adventurers, from history enthusiasts to nature lovers and film buffs. The combination of desert landscapes, unique cultural encounters, and the tranquility of the oasis makes Tozeur and the Chott El Jerid a truly extraordinary destination for anyone visiting Tunisia.

CHAPTER 3: CUISINE AND DINING

Must-Try Dishes

Tunisia's cuisine is a fascinating blend of Mediterranean, Arab, and Berber influences, offering a vibrant array of flavors that reflect the country's diverse history and cultural heritage. The dishes are rich in spices, fresh vegetables, seafood, and meats, creating meals that are both satisfying and full of character. For visitors to Tunisia, experiencing the local food is an essential part of the journey, as it provides an insight into the country's culinary traditions. Among the most iconic dishes are **couscous**, **brik**, **mechouia**, and others, each offering a unique taste of Tunisia's regional specialties.

Couscous is perhaps the most famous Tunisian dish and is a staple of the local diet. Made from steamed semolina wheat, couscous is served as the base of many traditional meals, typically paired with lamb, chicken, or fish, and accompanied by a variety of vegetables such as carrots, zucchini, and chickpeas. It is often flavored with spices like **cumin**, **coriander**, **turmeric**, and **harissa**—a fiery chili paste that is a hallmark of Tunisian cuisine. The dish is rich, hearty, and versatile, with each region in Tunisia offering its own variation. In the north, couscous is often prepared with seafood, while in the south, lamb or beef is more common.

The **nutritional value** of couscous is high, providing a good source of carbohydrates, fiber, and essential minerals like **iron** and **magnesium**. When combined with protein-rich meats and vegetables, couscous can serve as a well-balanced, nutritious meal. Many **top restaurants** in Tunisia, especially in cities like **Tunis**, **Sousse**, and **Monastir**, serve couscous in various styles. In Tunis, **Dar El Jeld** (5 Rue des Andalous, Tunis) is renowned for its traditional couscous, offering an upscale dining experience where you can enjoy lamb couscous served with a rich sauce. Another excellent spot is **El Walima** (8 Rue du Marché, Tunis), where couscous is prepared in authentic Tunisian style with an option for **seafood couscous**. The average price for a couscous dish in a mid-range restaurant typically ranges from **20-30 TND ($6-10 USD)**.

Another must-try dish is **brik**, a deep-fried pastry filled with a mixture of egg, tuna, capers, and parsley. This appetizer or snack is incredibly popular in Tunisia and is often served as a starter at many meals, especially during Ramadan and festive occasions. The pastry used for brik is **thin and crispy**, and it's typically served hot, making it an ideal choice for those looking for a savory, bite-sized treat. The **nutritional value** of brik is moderate, as it is high in protein from the egg and tuna but also rich in fats due to the frying process. Though brik is delicious, it should be eaten in moderation, especially for those concerned with their fat intake.

To taste the best brik, head to **Chez Slah** (Rue de la Kasbah, Tunis), a beloved local spot that's famous for serving some of the finest brik in the country. For a more laid-back, casual experience, visit **Le Restaurant de la Plage** in **Sousse**, where brik is often served as part of a larger seafood platter. Expect to pay around **5-10 TND ($2-3 USD)** for a single brik, which can be a light snack or appetizer before a main course.

Mechouia is another quintessential Tunisian dish that should not be missed. It is a traditional salad made with roasted tomatoes, peppers, onions, garlic, and olive oil, often topped with hard-boiled eggs, tuna, and olives. Mechouia is usually served as a side dish or appetizer and is particularly popular in the summer months due to its refreshing, light qualities. The smoky flavors from the roasted vegetables give it a distinct and unforgettable taste. In some variations, **harissa** is added to give it an extra spicy kick. It's typically eaten with **pita bread** or **French baguette**, allowing the soft, flavorful vegetables to be scooped up and savored.

For the best **mechouia**, head to **Le Tunisien** (Avenue Habib Bourguiba, Tunis), a charming bistro that offers traditional Tunisian salads, including mechouia. Another excellent restaurant serving mechouia is **Café des Délices** (15 Rue 2 Mars, Sousse), where the dish is accompanied by a variety of Tunisian flatbreads. The cost for a serving of mechouia in most restaurants is typically around **8-15 TND ($3-5 USD)**, making it an affordable and delicious starter. Nutritionally, mechouia is low in calories and fat but packed with vitamins from the vegetables, making it an excellent choice for those seeking a healthy, flavorful dish.

For something a little different, consider trying **Lablabi**, a flavorful chickpea soup that is a street food favorite in

Tunisia. It's typically served with a rich broth, pieces of **stale bread**, and spiced with **garlic, cumin, paprika**, and **harissa**. It's usually topped with a poached egg, adding extra protein to the dish. Lablabi is a common breakfast dish, but it can also be enjoyed as a hearty lunch or dinner. In terms of nutrition, lablabi is a fantastic source of protein from the chickpeas and egg, and it's also rich in fiber, which aids in digestion. As a warm, comforting meal, it's perfect for cooler months but enjoyed year-round.

To taste lablabi, visit **Le Petit Café** (Rue de la République, Tunis), a cozy, local spot that offers lablabi as one of their signature dishes. For a more rustic experience, try **Café El Mahaba** in **Tunis**, where this dish is served with generous portions and flavorful broth. A typical serving of lablabi costs around **6-10 TND ($2-3 USD)**.

Mechoui, a roasted lamb dish, is another Tunisian specialty that visitors should experience. It involves slow-cooking whole lambs over an open flame, resulting in tender meat that can be served with couscous, bread, or even as part of a **meze platter**. The dish is often enjoyed during special occasions and feasts. The lamb is usually flavored with aromatic spices such as **cumin, garlic**, and **coriander**, making each bite rich in flavor. As a high-protein, rich dish, it provides a satisfying meal. In Tunisia, **Mechoui** is typically served in **local restaurants** offering traditional Tunisian grilling and is usually priced around **25-50 TND ($8-15 USD)** per person, depending on the portion size and location.

For dessert, **Baklava** is a popular choice, a sweet pastry made of layers of **filo dough**, honey, and **pistachios** or

almonds. The **nutritional value** of baklava is relatively high in sugar and fat but provides energy, especially as an occasional indulgence. In Tunis, **Le Comptoir de Tunis** (10 Rue El Kasbah, Tunis) serves a decadent version of baklava that pairs wonderfully with a cup of **mint tea**, which is often served after meals. A slice of baklava here costs around **5 TND ($1.50 USD)**.

When dining in Tunisia, you will also find a variety of **fresh seafood**, especially in coastal cities like **Sousse**, **Monastir**, and **Hammamet**, where **grilled fish**, **octopus**, and **shrimp** dishes are common. These are often paired with sides of **vegetables** or **couscous** for a balanced meal.

From hearty couscous to crispy brik, flavorful mechouia, and comforting lablabi, the food in Tunisia is both delicious and affordable, making it an integral part of any travel experience. The country's many local eateries, bistros, and upscale restaurants provide ample opportunities to sample these dishes, with prices generally ranging from **5-30 TND ($2-10 USD)** for most traditional meals. Whether you're enjoying a casual street food snack or indulging in a multi-course meal, the rich flavors and fresh ingredients will leave a lasting impression.

Local Markets & Street Food

In Tunisia, **local markets**—known as **souks**—are an integral part of the country's cultural fabric, offering visitors a vivid snapshot of daily life, history, and the diversity of Tunisian goods. These bustling markets are where centuries-old traditions and vibrant modern commerce intersect. Here, shoppers can find everything from **spices, handmade crafts**, and **textiles** to fresh produce, **jewelry**, and local street food. Each city in Tunisia boasts its own unique souk, but some of the most famous ones are located in **Tunis, Sousse, Kairouan**, and **Sfax**.

The Medina of Tunis is one of the most famous souks in Tunisia, offering an incredible mix of historical architecture and commercial activity. Situated in the heart of the capital, the **Medina** is a UNESCO World Heritage site filled with narrow, winding alleys that open into bustling market squares. Here, visitors can explore the **Souk el Attarine**, which specializes in **spices, perfumes**, and **incense**, often sold by local vendors who are more than happy to share the history and uses of each fragrant product. The **Souk el Jomaa** is another part of the Medina famous for its variety of **textiles**, including **woolen rugs, scarves**, and **tunisian-made garments**. The **Souk des Chechias**, located close to the Medina, is where you'll find the traditional **chechia**, the red felt hat synonymous with Tunisian culture. The average cost of a **chechia** ranges from **20-50 TND ($7-17 USD)**, depending on the quality and craftsmanship. You can easily get to the Medina by taking a taxi from any major hotel in

Tunis, or via the **TGM (Tunis-Goulette-Marsa)** commuter train.

In terms of food, the **Medina of Tunis** has plenty to offer. The **street food stalls** near the souks are filled with locals grabbing a quick bite during their busy days. One of the most popular options is **makroud**, a semolina-based pastry filled with dates and fried to perfection, often coated in syrup. It's a favorite snack to enjoy on the go. A portion of **makroud** typically costs about **2-5 TND ($1-2 USD)**. Another beloved street food is **bambalouni**, a fried dough pastry sprinkled with powdered sugar. Street vendors sell these in the Medina for around **1-3 TND ($0.30-1 USD)**.

If you're looking for a more local market experience outside of the capital, **Sousse**'s **Medina** is equally captivating. The souk in Sousse is filled with a mix of **tourist trinkets** and authentic **artisan products**, ranging from **ceramics**, **pottery**, **leather goods**, and **wooden carvings** to **handmade jewelry**. One notable find is **Sousse's pottery**, famous for its intricate designs and vibrant colors. A beautiful piece of pottery or ceramic work will generally cost around **20-50 TND ($7-17 USD)**, but prices can go higher for larger, more elaborate items. The **Sousse Medina** is easily accessible from the city center or by taxi. As you wander, be sure to also look out for **local spices**, particularly **cumin**, **coriander**, and the all-important **harissa**, Tunisia's iconic hot chili paste.

For street food lovers, Sousse has its own collection of small food carts that line the streets near the **Ribat** (the historical fort). Popular dishes include **brik**, a crisp pastry filled with egg, tuna, and parsley, which is widely available in small food stalls across Sousse. **Brik** usually costs about **5-7 TND ($2-3 USD)**, making it an affordable yet satisfying snack. In addition to brik, **lablabi**—a spicy chickpea soup with bread, garlic, and cumin—is commonly sold by street vendors in Sousse and costs around **4-7 TND ($1.5-2.5 USD)** per bowl.

For those venturing to **Kairouan**, another important city steeped in history and culture, the souk is filled with **fine carpets** and **handwoven textiles**. Kairouan is known for its high-quality **woolen rugs**, which are crafted by local artisans using traditional methods passed down through generations. These rugs are a prized souvenir for visitors, with prices ranging from **50 TND ($17 USD)** for small, simple designs to over **500 TND ($170 USD)** for larger, more intricate pieces. The souk in Kairouan is also a great place to pick up **local sweets**, such as **baklava** or **sfiha**, a type of shortbread cookie filled with almond paste. A box of these local sweets might cost around **10-20 TND ($3-7 USD)**.

Sfax, Tunisia's second-largest city, offers another vibrant market experience. The souks here tend to be less touristy and more geared toward locals, which gives them an authentic, bustling atmosphere. **Sfax's souk el Medina** is a great place to shop for local olive oil, which is a major export of Tunisia, as well as fresh produce and handwoven baskets. **Tunisia's olive oil** is one of the finest in the world, and a liter of premium quality can cost anywhere from **15-30 TND ($5-10 USD)** depending on the grade and origin. Visitors to Sfax can also explore the **traditional leather**

market where the iconic **Tunisian slippers**—called **babouches**—are sold for around **20-40 TND ($7-14 USD)**.

In terms of street food, **Sfax** offers plenty of delicious local dishes. You'll find **grilled meats**, such as **brochettes** (skewered lamb or chicken) and **mechoui** (roast lamb), served at food carts and local eateries. These meats are usually seasoned with **spices** and served with bread and fresh salad. A skewer of **brochettes** typically costs **5-10 TND ($2-3 USD)**, while a plate of **mechoui** can go for around **15-25 TND ($5-9 USD)**.

The experience of exploring Tunisia's souks and tasting its street food is a delightful sensory journey, offering an opportunity to interact with locals, discover artisanal products, and enjoy delicious, fresh dishes. Bargaining is common practice in these markets, so it's always advisable to engage in a bit of haggling, especially when purchasing souvenirs like carpets, pottery, and textiles. It's important to be mindful of your budget as prices can vary significantly depending on the location and the vendor's perspective of a tourist's willingness to pay.

Visiting the souks and enjoying the street food is an essential experience for any traveler to Tunisia. It's not just about shopping or eating—it's about immersing yourself in the lively, colorful atmosphere of Tunisia's heart and soul. Whether you're enjoying a refreshing glass of **fresh orange juice**, savoring a **bambalouni**, or bargaining for a beautifully crafted rug, the local markets and street food in Tunisia offer an authentic and unforgettable experience that will stay with you long after you've left.

Wine and Mint Tea

These two beverages embody the warmth, history, and flavor of Tunisia, each with its unique characteristics and cultural significance. Tunisia, though predominantly a Muslim country, has a long history of wine production, dating back to the **Phoenician** and **Roman** periods. Mint tea, on the other hand, is a staple of Tunisian hospitality, a refreshing and aromatic drink that's consumed throughout the day, often as a symbol of warmth and welcome. Both drinks play a central role in the Tunisian social scene, whether sipped slowly in a café or shared among friends in a bustling market.

Tunisian wine has a rich and diverse history, shaped by the country's Mediterranean climate, which is ideal for grape cultivation. Tunisia's wine-growing regions are mostly concentrated in the north, around the **Cap Bon Peninsula**, **Tunis**, and the **Sahel** area near **Sousse**. The country produces a variety of wines, ranging from **reds** and **whites** to **rosés**, each with its unique characteristics influenced by the terroir and local grape varieties. Among the most famous grape varieties used in Tunisia's winemaking process are **Cinsault, Syrah, Grenache**, and **Carignan**, which are grown alongside more traditional varieties like **Sauvignon Blanc** and **Chardonnay**. **Chardonnay** is particularly notable for its popularity among white wine drinkers, offering a crisp, fresh flavor with citrus undertones. For red wines, **Cinsault** is particularly beloved for its light body, offering a smooth taste with fruity and spicy notes.

Tunisia's wine industry has grown significantly in recent years, with some wineries gaining international recognition for their high-quality production. One of the best-known Tunisian wineries is **Domaine Neferis**, located near the city of **Mornag** in the **Cap Bon** region. The winery produces a variety of wines, including red, white, and rosé, with one of their standout offerings being the **Neferis Reserve**, a robust red wine made from **Syrah** and **Cinsault** grapes. Visitors can tour the vineyard and participate in tastings, which typically cost around **30-50 TND ($10-17 USD)** per person, depending on the package. To get there, you can take a taxi or rent a car from **Tunis** (about a 30-minute drive), and it's advisable to book a tour in advance. For those staying in **Sousse**, **Domaine Bouchemma**, another respected winery located near the city, also offers guided tours and tastings of their range of Tunisian wines. The average cost of a bottle of local wine in restaurants typically ranges from **25-60 TND ($8-20 USD)**, though boutique wines and premium selections can reach much higher prices.

Tunisian wine is often served with local cuisine, particularly with dishes like **couscous, grilled meats**, and **seafood**, where the wine complements the spices and rich flavors of the food. Whether you're in a high-end restaurant or a casual café, local wine is almost always available, and it pairs perfectly with traditional meals. In **Tunis**, the **Dar El Jeld** restaurant (5 Rue des Andalous, Tunis) is one of the best places to enjoy a glass of Tunisian wine. The restaurant offers an extensive wine list, including several selections from local vineyards, and provides an intimate setting for those wishing to experience the rich culture of

Tunisian dining. Prices for a glass of wine here typically range from **8-15 TND ($3-5 USD)**.

Another place where visitors can savor Tunisian wine is at **Le Comptoir de Tunis** (Avenue Habib Bourguiba, Tunis), a bistro-style restaurant that serves a selection of wines from Tunisia's top vineyards. The restaurant offers a cozy atmosphere for wine enthusiasts to sample both local and international wines, paired with an assortment of appetizers. A glass of Tunisian wine here usually costs around **10-20 TND ($3-7 USD)**.

While Tunisian wine has a long history, **mint tea** is arguably the most iconic beverage in Tunisia, enjoyed by locals and visitors alike. This refreshing, aromatic tea is made from **green tea**, fresh **mint leaves**, and sugar, and it's typically served in small glasses, often accompanied by small sweets or pastries. Mint tea is a key part of Tunisian hospitality, and it's offered to guests in homes, cafés, and restaurants as a gesture of friendship and warmth. The ritual of drinking mint tea is often social, with people gathering around in cafés or private homes to chat, relax, and enjoy the drink. In many ways, it's a symbol of the country's tradition of hospitality.

The preparation of mint tea in Tunisia is an art form in itself. While it may seem simple, the perfect cup requires the right balance of sugar and mint. The tea itself is typically brewed strong and sweet, with fresh mint added to enhance the fragrance and flavor. It is often served in **small glass cups** that are about half the size of a typical coffee mug, making it easy to sip throughout a leisurely conversation. You'll find that the sweetness of the tea is often adjusted according to personal preference, with some opting for a lighter touch while others enjoy it quite sweet.

Mint tea can be found throughout Tunisia in various settings, from street vendors to upscale restaurants. In **Tunis**, **Café des Délices** (15 Rue de la Kasbah, Tunis) is a popular spot for a traditional cup of mint tea. This café, with its charming atmosphere and panoramic views of the city, is ideal for sipping mint tea while watching the hustle and bustle of daily life unfold. A glass of mint tea here costs around **2-4 TND ($1-1.5 USD)**. Another great option in the city is **Le Café du Théâtre** (Avenue Habib Bourguiba, Tunis), where you can enjoy mint tea along with pastries while people-watching on the vibrant avenue. A glass of mint tea here typically costs **2-3 TND ($0.70-1 USD)**.

In the **coastal town of Sousse**, **Café El Mahaba** (Sousse Medina, Sousse) offers visitors a warm, traditional setting to enjoy mint tea. Situated in the heart of the Medina, this café serves mint tea with a local touch, often accompanied by **makroud**, the sweet semolina pastry. The cost for a glass of mint tea here is around **2-4 TND ($0.70-1.5 USD)**.

Beyond its delightful taste, mint tea is also known for its **health benefits**. The fresh mint leaves help with digestion, and the tea itself is often consumed after meals to soothe the stomach and refresh the senses. Moreover, mint tea's calming properties make it a perfect way to unwind after a long day of exploring Tunisia's historic sites and vibrant souks.

In Tunisia, it's common to enjoy mint tea with **pastries** or **sweets**. For a truly local experience, look for cafes or restaurants that serve it alongside **baklava** or **bambalouni** (fried dough pastries). **Bambalouni**, a popular street food, is often served warm, dusted with powdered sugar, and is a great companion to a cup of mint tea.

For those wishing to take a piece of Tunisia's beverage culture home, **mint tea** is widely available in supermarkets and local markets, often packaged in loose-leaf form or in pre-packaged tea bags. Some brands even sell specialty mint blends that combine traditional green tea with other herbs and flavors.

Tunisian wine and mint tea offer visitors a chance to experience the country's rich culinary traditions, from the **vineyards** of Cap Bon to the cafés of Tunis. Whether you're enjoying a fine glass of **Neferis Reserve** in a sophisticated restaurant or sipping a sweet cup of mint tea at a street café, these drinks provide an authentic taste of Tunisia's hospitality, history, and flavor. The relatively low cost of both wine and mint tea makes them accessible to all travelers, and their availability in almost every corner of the country means that they can easily be enjoyed by anyone looking to relax, socialize, and explore the local culture.

Dining Etiquette & Where to Eat

Dining etiquette in Tunisia is an essential aspect of the country's rich cultural fabric, and understanding the local customs will help visitors fully immerse themselves in the experience. Tunisian dining is typically a **social affair**, often shared with friends and family, where meals are eaten together and served in a communal fashion. It's common to see people sitting around a large table, enjoying the food in a relaxed atmosphere. The food culture reflects Tunisia's history, with influences from **Arab**, **Mediterranean**, **French**, and **Berber** traditions, making the country a fantastic destination for food lovers.

When dining in Tunisia, there are several customs and practices that visitors should be mindful of. First and foremost, it's customary to wait for the host to begin eating before starting your meal, as a sign of respect. You will often be served first, particularly if you are a guest, and it is polite to accept the first serving. In Tunisia, **sharing food** is a significant part of the dining experience, and it's common for large platters of food to be passed around for everyone to partake in. Typically, meals are eaten with the **right hand**, as the left hand is considered less clean, and it's best to avoid using it for food. For formal occasions, people may use utensils, but in many traditional settings, food is eaten with **bread** or even the fingers, especially for dishes like **couscous** or **lablabi** (chickpea soup). **Bread** is often used as a scoop or utensil, making it a central part of the meal.

Tunisian cuisine, with its use of **spices** and fresh ingredients, is known for its bold flavors and hearty dishes. **Couscous** is a staple, typically served with lamb, chicken, or vegetables, and accompanied by a rich sauce made with spices like cumin, coriander, and saffron. Another popular dish is **brik**, a crispy pastry filled with egg, tuna, and capers, deep-fried to golden perfection. **Mechoui**, a type of roasted lamb, is another favorite, often prepared for special occasions or large gatherings.

The major cities in Tunisia offer a diverse range of dining options, from **traditional eateries** to more contemporary, high-end restaurants. **Tunis**, the capital, is home to a wide variety of dining experiences, with several establishments offering both traditional Tunisian dishes and international cuisine.

In **Tunis**, one of the best places to sample local Tunisian cuisine is **Dar El Jeld** (5 Rue des Andalous, Tunis). Located in the heart of the **Medina**, this restaurant offers a refined dining experience in an elegant, historic setting. It specializes in traditional Tunisian dishes such as **lablabi**, **couscous**, and **mechoui**, as well as a selection of **seafood** dishes, including **grilled fish**. The average cost for a three-course meal here is approximately **40-70 TND ($13-24 USD)** per person. Dar El Jeld is not only known for its food but also for its beautiful decor, which is representative of traditional Tunisian architecture. To get there, you can take a taxi from central Tunis or a local bus, but be sure to check the bus routes in advance, as they can be difficult to navigate for newcomers.

For a more contemporary dining experience in Tunis, **Le Comptoir de Tunis** (Avenue Habib Bourguiba, Tunis) offers a more modern atmosphere with a selection of both local and international dishes. The menu includes Tunisian **grilled meats**, **tagines**, and a range of **pastas** and **salads**. The restaurant also boasts a good selection of wines, including some locally produced options. The average cost for a meal here is around **30-50 TND ($10-17 USD)** per person, and it's an excellent spot for a relaxed evening meal or a drink with friends. You can easily reach **Le Comptoir de Tunis** by taking a taxi or using the **TGM commuter train** from the downtown area.

In **Sousse**, located on the eastern coast of Tunisia, there's a wealth of **seafood restaurants** thanks to its coastal location. One of the best seafood spots in the city is **La Bouillabaisse** (Boulevard de l'Environnement, Sousse), a well-known restaurant offering an extensive menu focused on fresh fish and shellfish. **Bouillabaisse** (a traditional Mediterranean fish stew) is a standout dish here, along with grilled fish and **seafood couscous**. The cost of a meal at **La Bouillabaisse** typically ranges from **30-50 TND ($10-17 USD)** per person, depending on the selection of seafood. To get there, visitors can easily walk from the **Sousse Medina** or take a short taxi ride from any of the central hotels.

For something a bit more relaxed, **Le Prince** (Avenue de la République, Sousse) is a favorite among locals for **street food** and **grilled meats**. Known for its **shish kebabs**, **mechoui**, and **brik**, this casual eatery offers a variety of Tunisian specialties at a lower cost. The average meal here costs about **15-25 TND ($5-9 USD)**. It's a great spot to enjoy a traditional Tunisian lunch or dinner in a cozy and informal environment.

In **Djerba**, an island located off the southern coast of Tunisia, seafood is also a prominent part of the local cuisine. **Chez Ali** (Midoun, Djerba), one of the island's most famous restaurants, serves an array of fresh seafood dishes along with classic Tunisian dishes like **couscous** and **mechoui**. Visitors here rave about the **lobster, grilled fish**, and the **fish soup**, and the ambiance is always lively with musicians playing traditional tunes in the background. The average cost for a full meal at **Chez Ali** is about **40-60 TND ($13-20 USD)**. You can easily reach the restaurant by taking a taxi from **Houmt Souk**, the main town of Djerba, which is about a 30-minute drive away.

For a more upscale experience on Djerba, **La Mer** (Hotel Radisson Blu, Djerba) offers a fine dining experience with views of the Mediterranean. It specializes in **tunisian Mediterranean fusion** dishes, mixing local ingredients like olive oil, seafood, and spices with international techniques. The atmosphere is elegant, making it a great spot for a romantic dinner or special occasion. A meal at **La Mer** typically costs around **60-90 TND ($20-30 USD)** per person, and it's advisable to book a table in advance, especially during the peak tourist season. You can reach this restaurant by taking a taxi from any of the main hotels on Djerba Island.

In **Kairouan**, one of Tunisia's most historic cities, traditional Tunisian food can be found in numerous local eateries. A notable spot is **Restaurant el-Ayachi** (Medina,

Kairouan), where visitors can enjoy classic dishes like **couscous**, **lablabi**, and **mechoui**. Kairouan is also famous for its **sweets**, particularly **makroud**, a semolina pastry filled with dates and almonds. A meal here generally costs between **20-40 TND ($7-13 USD)** per person. The restaurant is located in the heart of the Medina, and taxis can easily get you there from the city center.

Dining etiquette in Tunisia also involves respect for the local culture and customs. For instance, in more traditional or family-run restaurants, it's considered impolite to rush through a meal. Dining is a leisurely process, often lasting several hours, with ample time spent chatting and enjoying the food. **Compliments** about the food are often appreciated, and it's common to offer praise for the host or the chef. When dining in a larger group, it's also customary to offer to share your food with others.

Whether you're eating at a **high-end restaurant** or grabbing a quick bite at a **local café**, Tunisia offers an array of dining options for all budgets and tastes. With its rich history, welcoming atmosphere, and delicious food, Tunisia is a place where food becomes more than just a necessity—it's an experience to be savored and shared.

CHAPTER 4: CULTURAL EXPERIENCES

Festivals

Tunisian festivals offer an extraordinary glimpse into the country's vibrant culture, arts, and history. These celebrations not only showcase Tunisia's rich traditions but also its modern influences and aspirations. From the enchanting rhythms of **traditional music festivals** to the glitz and glamour of **international film festivals**, there's something to excite every visitor throughout the year. Among the most significant and internationally recognized events are the **International Film Festival of Carthage (JCC)** and the **Carthage Film Festival**, which together draw thousands of visitors, filmmakers, artists, and cinephiles from all over the world.

The **Carthage Film Festival (Festival International de Carthage)** is Tunisia's oldest and most prestigious cultural event. First held in **1966**, this festival celebrates cinema in all its forms and is a major player in the **African and Arab film industry**. It's held in **Tunis**, the capital of Tunisia, usually in **October** every two years, and runs for about a week. The festival aims to promote cinematic expression and provide a platform for filmmakers from the Arab world, Africa, and other regions to showcase their works. The festival is an eclectic blend of **feature films**, **documentaries**, **short films**, and **animated films**, each exploring various cultural, social, and political themes.

The festival takes place at **Carthage Theatre** (Avenue Mohamed V, Tunis), a grand venue located in the heart of Tunis, offering a charming backdrop for screenings. The festival is renowned for its inclusive nature, embracing **international films** while prioritizing works from **North Africa** and the **Arab world**. Visitors can expect to see stunning works of cinema that offer thought-provoking commentary on modern-day issues such as **identity**, **migration**, **political change**, and **gender equality**. The festival also includes **workshops** and **panels** where filmmakers can engage in discussions, and film lovers can deepen their understanding of the world of cinema. The **entry fee** for screenings typically ranges between **5-10 TND ($2-3 USD)** per film, while some screenings may be free, depending on the event. Tickets can be purchased at the venue or through the official festival website. Given the nature of the event, it's best to **book tickets in advance**, especially for highly anticipated films.

For film buffs, one of the most exciting aspects of the festival is the **competition section**, where the best films in various categories (such as Best Arab Film, Best African Film, and Best Documentary) are awarded prestigious prizes. These accolades bring global attention to filmmakers and often serve as a springboard for their international careers. The **audience** also plays a key role in the festival, with opportunities to engage with the filmmakers, actors, and other industry professionals during the **post-screening Q&A sessions**. The **age restriction** for attending films varies by film, but typically, films are rated for general audiences, with some films containing mature content that may have an age limit of 18+.

Another major cultural event in Tunisia is the **International Festival of Carthage (Festival International de Carthage)**, which is often held annually in **July** or **August**. This festival focuses on **music** and **theater** and is set in the stunning **Roman ruins of Carthage** (located just outside **Tunis**), offering an unparalleled experience where visitors can enjoy world-class performances against the backdrop of ancient history. The **Carthage Festival** spans about three weeks, and performances include concerts by **international music legends**, **local bands**, and **traditional Tunisian ensembles**. Artists from around the world come to perform across a variety of genres, including **classical music**, **jazz**, **pop**, **rock**, **electronic**, and **folk**.

Held in the **Carthage Amphitheater**, an iconic historical site, the festival brings together a fusion of **Tunisia's rich cultural heritage** and modern global art. The unique setting, coupled with the magical ambiance of the Mediterranean evening air, makes it one of the most captivating music festivals in the region. The **entry fee** for most concerts generally ranges from **30-50 TND ($10-17 USD)**, depending on the artist or the performance's prestige. Tickets are available at the **Carthage Festival Box Office** (Carthage Theatre, Tunis), but it's also worth checking for online availability. Given the popularity of the event, especially during the summer months, booking tickets in advance is advisable.

In addition to the performances, the **International Festival of Carthage** also includes **dance performances**, **theater productions**, and **art exhibitions**, creating a multifaceted cultural event. Visitors will enjoy seeing a wide range of artistic expressions, from **traditional Tunisian folk dances** and **flamenco performances** to **theater productions** that blend **modern themes** with **classical storytelling**. Local Tunisian artists also have the opportunity to showcase their talents, offering a great opportunity for visitors to discover the thriving contemporary art scene in Tunisia. The festival attracts a mix of **locals** and **international tourists**, making it a vibrant and cosmopolitan event. Children and adults alike are welcomed, with some family-friendly performances and activities geared toward younger audiences.

If you're interested in **Tunisian music**, the **Carthage Festival** offers the perfect chance to experience the sounds of **local genres** such as **malouf** (classical Arabic music), **raï**, and **sufi music**, which hold a special place in the country's cultural identity. International stars also perform at the festival, with artists from the **Middle East**, **Africa**, and **Europe**, ensuring there is something for every music lover to enjoy.

In addition to the **film** and **music festivals**, Tunisia also hosts other cultural events that bring together **local** and **international participants**. For example, **The Festival of the Sahara** in **Douz** is a celebration of desert life, with camel races, **traditional Bedouin music**, and **poetry readings**, as well as a showcase of **local crafts** and **gastronomy**. This festival is typically held in **December** and offers a unique chance to explore Tunisia's desert culture, far away from the bustling cities.

The **Festival of the Medina**, another significant cultural event, takes place in **Tunis** and focuses on showcasing Tunisia's **artistic heritage** through various forms, including **visual arts, theater**, and **dance**. It's held in the heart of the **Medina of Tunis**, a UNESCO World Heritage site, and allows visitors to experience performances in some of the city's most beautiful and historic locations.

Visitors to Tunisia should also keep an eye out for smaller festivals and local events that take place in various cities throughout the year, such as **the Sousse Festival, the Bizerte Music Festival**, and **the Kairouan International Festival**, all of which offer a glimpse into Tunisia's rich and diverse cultural offerings.

To fully enjoy Tunisia's festivals, it's best to plan your trip around one or more of these events. Getting to most festivals is relatively easy, as they are typically held in well-known locations like **Tunis**, **Carthage**, **Sousse**, and **Douz**, all of which are accessible by **public transportation, taxis**, or **car rentals**. If you plan to visit during peak festival seasons, it's also important to book accommodation well in advance, as these events attract large crowds, and hotels can fill up quickly. Many visitors choose to stay in **Tunis**, which offers a variety of accommodations ranging from budget options to more luxurious hotels, as it is centrally located and provides easy access to most cultural events.

Tunisia's festivals are an excellent way for visitors to experience the country's **diverse culture**, **history**, and **modern artistic expressions**. Whether you're attending the **Carthage Film Festival**, enjoying the **International**

Festival of Carthage, or discovering other regional celebrations, Tunisia's festivals offer something for every type of traveler, from film lovers to music enthusiasts and beyond. The festivals create an opportunity for cultural exchange, and they remain a testament to Tunisia's enduring heritage and creativity.

Mosques, Churches & Synagogues

These sacred sites are not only places of worship but also offer visitors a unique opportunity to explore Tunisia's rich **history, architecture**, and **interfaith coexistence**. From the **stunning mosques** that dominate the skyline to **historic synagogues** and **ancient churches**, Tunisia's religious landmarks provide insight into the diverse cultures and religious traditions that have shaped the country.

Among the most important mosques in Tunisia is the **Zitouna Mosque** in **Tunis**, located in the heart of the **Medina**. Dating back to the **8th century**, the Zitouna Mosque is one of the oldest and most significant in North Africa. It was founded in **698 CE** and served as a prominent center for **Islamic learning** and jurisprudence. Its name, "Zitouna," refers to the **olive trees** that once surrounded the mosque, adding to its tranquil atmosphere. Visitors can admire the mosque's **grand architecture**, which blends **Arab-Islamic** design with **local Tunisian** influences. Its massive courtyard, adorned with **arches** and

intricate tilework, offers a serene place to sit and reflect. The mosque's **minaret** stands as a symbol of Tunis' Islamic heritage and dominates the skyline. While the mosque is still active as a place of worship, non-Muslim visitors are usually allowed access to certain parts of the mosque, such as the courtyard, but access to the prayer hall is typically restricted. The mosque is open for visitors **from 9 AM to 5 PM**, with no entry fee. To reach the **Zitouna Mosque**, visitors can easily get to **Tunis Medina** by walking from **Habib Bourguiba Avenue** or by taking a taxi, which is a convenient option for those unfamiliar with the city's narrow streets.

Another important mosque is the **Great Mosque of Kairouan** in the city of **Kairouan**, which is one of the holiest cities in the Islamic world and a UNESCO World Heritage Site. This mosque is considered a masterpiece of **Islamic architecture** and was built in **670 CE**. The **Great Mosque of Kairouan** has long been a significant religious and intellectual center for **Sunni Muslims**. The mosque features a stunning array of **Islamic art**, including its famous **arched galleries**, **intricate stucco work**, and its **famous prayer hall**. It also boasts a beautiful **courtyard**, where visitors can admire the stone columns and admire the surrounding **olive trees**. One of the most captivating aspects of the mosque is its **minaret**, which stands as a monumental structure and is a beacon for travelers arriving in Kairouan. There is no **entry fee** to the mosque, but donations are often welcomed. Visitors can take a **taxi** or **bus** to **Kairouan**, which is about **2.5 hours by car** from **Tunis**. The mosque is open to visitors from **9 AM to 5 PM**, but it is important to dress modestly when visiting, as it is still a functioning place of worship.

For those interested in **Christian history**, Tunisia offers several stunning churches, with the **Cathedral of St. Vincent de Paul** in Tunis being a prime example. Located on **Habib Bourguiba Avenue**, this **neo-gothic cathedral** was built during the **French colonial period** and stands as a symbol of Tunisia's Christian minority. The cathedral's striking architecture, with its tall spires and colorful stained glass windows, is one of the most impressive in the country. Though it is not as old as some of the other religious sites, the cathedral is still an important place of **worship** and is often used for **mass** and **religious events**. Visitors to the **Cathedral of St. Vincent de Paul** can admire its **Gothic design**, featuring **twin towers**, **ornate arches**, and stunning **interior mosaics**. The **church** is open to visitors **from 9 AM to 6 PM**, and admission is generally free, though a small donation is encouraged. Visitors can easily reach the cathedral by walking from **Tunis' central downtown area**, or they can take a **taxi** to the church, which is easily accessible by public transport.

In the historic town of **Djerba**, which is known for its **Jewish heritage**, the **El Ghriba Synagogue** stands as one of the oldest and most significant synagogues in the world. The synagogue is located in the town of **Erriadh**, and it has been a center of Jewish worship for over **2,000 years**. It holds special significance for both **Jewish** and **Muslim** communities, as it has long been a place of **pilgrimage**. The El Ghriba Synagogue is renowned for its **beautiful architecture**, with whitewashed walls, intricate carvings, and colorful **mosaics**. Its courtyard is adorned with symbolic objects, and visitors can learn about the synagogue's rich history, particularly its role in **Jewish-Muslim relations** in Tunisia. The synagogue hosts an annual **pilgrimage** during the **Lag BaOmer festival**, attracting visitors from around the world. The **synagogue** is open to visitors daily, and entry is usually free, but visitors are encouraged to leave a donation. The synagogue is located near **Houmt Souk**, the main town of Djerba, and can be easily reached by **taxi** or **bus** from various parts of the island. The visit is an opportunity to witness Tunisia's enduring commitment to religious tolerance, where **Jews**, **Muslims**, and **Christians** have coexisted peacefully for centuries.

The **Medina of Tunis** is home to a number of smaller **mosques** and **religious sites**, including the **Sidi Mahrez Mosque** and the **Sidi Youssef Mosque**. These mosques, like many others in Tunisia, are rich in **Islamic art** and **architecture**, featuring stunning **tilework**, **stucco decorations**, and peaceful courtyards. Visitors to the **Medina** should also make time to explore the **Bardo Museum**, which houses **artifacts** from Tunisia's diverse religious past, showcasing pieces related to **Roman**, **Islamic**, **Christian**, and **Jewish** history.

When visiting these religious sites, it is important to respect local customs and dress modestly. Women are generally expected to cover their shoulders and knees, and in some mosques, women may be required to wear a **headscarf**. Visitors should also be mindful of the fact that many mosques, synagogues, and churches are still active places of worship. Therefore, **visitors should be quiet** and **respectful**, especially during prayer times. Some mosques may also close temporarily during prayer, so it's worth planning your visit accordingly.

Tunisia's mosques, churches, and synagogues offer a captivating window into the country's rich religious heritage. Whether you're exploring the grand **Zitouna Mosque** in Tunis, the **Great Mosque of Kairouan**, or the **El Ghriba Synagogue** on Djerba, these religious landmarks offer an opportunity to experience Tunisia's diverse **spiritual traditions**. With a commitment to preserving and showcasing the country's diverse religious history, Tunisia provides a welcoming atmosphere for visitors seeking to learn more about the cultural and spiritual legacy of this fascinating country.

Spending Your Day in a Traditional Tunisian Home

A day in a traditional Tunisian home is an immersive experience in **warmth**, **generosity**, and the profound cultural importance of hospitality. Tunisia, with its rich **Arab**, **Berber**, **Ottoman**, and **French** influences, places a high value on family, respect for guests, and the sharing of food and stories. Visitors lucky enough to be invited into a local home will experience firsthand the beauty of **Tunisia's hospitality**, which is considered not only a cultural norm but a cherished tradition passed down through generations.

The day typically begins with a sense of **calm** and **warmth** that extends throughout the home. Tunisian homes are generally centered around a shared living space where family members spend much of their time. In many homes, the central room is a cozy **sitting area**, furnished with **plush cushions** and **low coffee tables**, creating a setting for conversation, tea, and meals. Visitors will often be greeted with a warm handshake and a heartfelt **"Marhaban"** or **"Ahilan wa sahlan"** (both expressions meaning "welcome"). Hospitality in Tunisia is an intrinsic part of the culture, and once inside, the atmosphere is immediately filled with a sense of **comfort** and **care**. The concept of being a good host is deeply woven into the fabric of Tunisian society, and it's common to see extended family members and friends gathering regularly to share food, celebrate life, and offer support.

After greeting, the first thing that a visitor will typically experience is the offering of **mint tea** or **coffee**. In many Tunisian homes, **mint tea**, known as **"atay bil na'na"**, is a ritual that transcends a simple beverage. It is a symbol of hospitality and is often served in delicate **glassware**. The preparation of mint tea is an elaborate process, beginning with the boiling of **green tea**, which is then poured into small glasses with **fresh mint leaves** and **sugar**. It's a delightful moment of pause as the host makes sure the guest feels welcomed and comfortable, offering a chance for conversation. Coffee, often prepared in the traditional **Turkish style**, is another common option, particularly if you're visiting in the morning or after lunch. Visitors will find that it's not only about the drink itself but the **ritual of offering** it, which is a gesture of respect and consideration.

As the day unfolds, you'll likely be invited to share a meal, which in Tunisia is often an event in itself. Lunch is usually the largest meal of the day and typically happens between **1 PM** and **3 PM**. Tunisian homes are renowned for the **generosity of their cooking**—dishes are often served in large portions, with the goal of ensuring that no guest leaves hungry. The dining table is usually a communal affair where everyone sits together to enjoy the food, and it's typical for family members and guests to share dishes. The most iconic dish in Tunisia is **couscous**, usually served with **lamb**, **chicken**, or **fish**, and accompanied by **vegetables** and a rich sauce. Visitors will also encounter **brik**, a fried pastry filled with **egg** and **tuna**, and **mechouia**, a salad made with **roasted peppers**, **tomatoes**, and **garlic**. The meal is often accompanied by fresh **bread**, typically baked locally and served warm, as well as **olives** and **olive oil**, which are integral to Tunisian cuisine.

Tunisian food is not just about flavors but also about the experience of eating together as a family. If you're a guest, you might notice that meals are often prepared with great care, using **fresh local ingredients** and recipes that have been passed down through generations. The preparation process might even be shared with you, with the host eagerly explaining how the dish is made or inviting you to help with small tasks. The connection between food, family, and culture is palpable, and the meal is often the highlight of the day's activities.

After lunch, it's common to rest for a bit, as the **Tunisian lifestyle** tends to be slow-paced during the afternoon heat. This period is known as the **"siesta"**, and it's when many families retreat to their private spaces or enjoy a quiet moment together. As the day cools down, visitors might be invited for an afternoon **walk around the neighborhood** or **tea time** on the **balcony** or **courtyard**. This is a wonderful time to relax and learn more about the **local life**. Families often live in homes with traditional **Arabesque-style courtyards**, with lush greenery and stone or tiled floors. These areas serve as both a place to entertain and a retreat from the heat of the day.

Tunisian homes are often decorated with local **craftsmanship**—from colorful **woven carpets** to hand-painted **tiles** and intricate **mosaic work**. The **architecture** of a traditional home often reflects the local culture, with high ceilings, expansive windows, and **cool stone walls** designed to keep the house cool during the **hot summer months**. As you relax and converse, you might hear stories about the family's history, Tunisia's **ancient traditions**, or even the broader history of the country itself. It's typical for older family members to share their knowledge of the country's customs, folklore, and even **Arabic poetry**. In these moments, you'll witness a deep respect for tradition and a profound connection between the present and the past.

If the visit takes place during a special occasion, such as a **wedding**, **birthday**, or **religious holiday** (like **Eid** or **Ramadan**), the level of celebration intensifies. For **Ramadan**, for instance, the evening meal called **Iftar** is an important family event. **Dates**, **soup**, and **bread** are the first foods served to break the fast, followed by larger meals featuring a range of **savory and sweet dishes**. The spirit of **togetherness** and **thankfulness** permeates these moments, and visitors may feel like they've been embraced into the heart of Tunisian life.

As the evening draws to a close, guests are often invited to enjoy some **desserts**, such as **baklava**, **makroud** (semolina cakes stuffed with dates and nuts), or **louza** (almond-based sweets), often accompanied by another round of tea. Throughout the day, guests are made to feel like part of the family, and this emphasis on sharing and connection is what makes Tunisian hospitality so remarkable. Whether visiting a modest home or a more affluent one, the **invitation into the home** signifies a deep sense of **trust** and **respect**.

Tunisian hospitality is not merely about offering food and drink—it is about cultivating relationships, exchanging stories, and fostering a deep sense of community. A day spent in a traditional Tunisian home will likely leave visitors with lasting memories of a **welcoming culture**, the **comfort of home-cooked meals**, and the realization that hospitality in Tunisia is not just a custom but a reflection of the country's values—where family, warmth, and generosity are paramount. Visitors will leave with a sense of having been embraced by the culture, having witnessed firsthand the **importance of human connection** and the incredible hospitality that defines Tunisian life.

Art and Craft Scene

Whether wandering through the bustling **souks** of Tunis, visiting artisan workshops in **Kairouan**, or admiring the colorful **textiles** of **Sidi Bou Said**, visitors will find themselves surrounded by a rich tapestry of artistic expression. Tunisia's crafts have been passed down through generations, with many artisans still using ancient techniques to create pieces that are both functional and decorative. The **souks** (markets), particularly in the old medinas, are an essential part of this world, offering visitors a glimpse into the country's ongoing love for traditional arts and crafts.

In the heart of cities like **Tunis, Kairouan,** and **Sousse**, the **souks** form a labyrinth of narrow streets and alleys where artisans proudly display their works. The word "souk" evokes the imagery of a **bustling market**, teeming with energy, color, and **handmade goods**. In these markets, visitors will encounter everything from intricately **embroidered textiles** to **metalwork, leather goods, woodwork,** and **jewelry**. The souks are not just places to shop but are also spaces where Tunisia's **crafting heritage** comes to life. Many of these goods are made by artisans whose families have been working in the same trade for generations. Watching a **blacksmith** hammering away at iron or a **carpet weaver** deftly maneuvering threads on a loom provides a window into the time-honored techniques that have been perfected over centuries.

One of the most popular crafts in Tunisia is **pottery**, which has deep historical significance in the region. The country's

pottery is typically made from **clay**, with artisans shaping it using age-old techniques. The most famous pottery comes from **Nabeul**, a town located on the northeastern coast of Tunisia. Nabeul is known for producing beautiful, brightly colored pottery that often features **geometric patterns, floral designs,** and **mosaic motifs**. Many visitors to Nabeul will find themselves wandering through small **workshops** where artisans create stunning plates, bowls, vases, and pitchers that showcase the intricate beauty of Tunisian design. The pottery is fired in traditional kilns and painted with natural **earth tones**, **cobalt blues**, and **bright reds** that represent Tunisia's vibrant landscapes and rich cultural history. Visitors to Nabeul can buy pieces directly from the workshops, and in many cases, they can watch the artisans at work, getting a deeper understanding of the craft.

In addition to pottery, **textiles** play a huge role in Tunisia's artistic scene, with some of the finest examples found in **traditional rugs** and **embroidered fabrics**. The country has a long history of textile production, with **wool**, **cotton**, and **silk** being woven into everything from **clothing** to **home decor**. Tunisia's famous **Berber carpets** are a highlight for visitors, particularly in towns like **Kairouan** and **Sousse**, where the tradition of **weaving** has been preserved over centuries. These carpets are often handwoven on **loom**, with designs that tell stories of **ancient traditions** and **tribal symbols**. The patterns can vary depending on the region but often feature **diamond shapes, geometric figures,** and **nature-inspired motifs**. The rich, earthy colors of these carpets are achieved through the use of natural dyes, and each piece is a reflection of the personal touch of the artisan.

Tunisian **embroidery** is another form of **traditional textile art** that can be found throughout the country. Highly detailed and painstakingly done by hand, embroidery often adorns **clothing, scarves,** and **tablecloths**. In particular, **Sidi Bou Said**, the charming blue-and-white village perched above the Mediterranean Sea, is known for its finely crafted **textiles**, including **shawls, pashminas,** and **embroidered dresses**. Many visitors come to this village specifically for its exquisite textiles, and a walk through the village's narrow, picturesque streets will often reveal small **workshops** where artisans use **traditional needlework** to create their designs. These fabrics often feature intricate patterns inspired by the region's nature, such as floral designs, **palm leaves,** and **geometric shapes**. Some artisans still use **natural dyes** derived from **plants** and **minerals**, preserving ancient techniques that have been passed down for generations.

The **souks** in cities like **Tunis** are also excellent places to shop for high-quality **leather goods**, another traditional craft. The **Tunisian leather** is famous for its durability and its rich textures, and the finest products come from the **medina** in **Tunis**. Leather artisans produce a range of goods, from **bags** and **belts** to **shoes** and **jackets**, often in earthy tones such as **brown, tan,** and **camel**. These leather items are usually hand-stitched, showcasing a level of craftsmanship that is rare in today's mass-produced world. Leather goods are often sold in the souks, where customers can haggle over prices, adding to the authenticity of the shopping experience. Prices for leather goods can vary, but visitors can expect to pay anywhere from **30 to 100 Tunisian Dinars** for a well-made piece, depending on size and complexity.

Tunisian **metalwork** is another highly regarded art form, particularly in **Sfax** and **Tunis**, where **brass** and **silver** are crafted into stunning **jewelry** and **decorative items**. One of the most famous metalworking traditions is the creation of **jewel-encrusted** pieces, often designed with motifs inspired by Tunisia's ancient history. Traditional **bracelets**, **necklaces**, and **earrings** are made with intricate details, often combining **gemstones** with **silver** or **gold**. The souks of **Tunis** offer a wonderful opportunity for visitors to purchase **unique, handcrafted jewelry** that captures the beauty of Tunisian craftsmanship.

To get the best of Tunisia's **art and craft scene**, visitors should make time to explore the **souks** and **artisan workshops** scattered throughout the country. For a particularly immersive experience, **Nabeul** is a must-visit destination for those interested in pottery, while **Sidi Bou Said** offers some of the finest **textiles** and **embroidered items**. The **Medina of Tunis** is also an essential stop for those who want to explore the full breadth of Tunisia's **traditional crafts**, from **pottery** to **metalwork** and **leather goods**. Bargaining is common in the markets, and visitors can expect to haggle with sellers over prices, which adds to the experience. Visitors are encouraged to **engage with the artisans**, many of whom are happy to share the stories behind their crafts, explaining the techniques they use and the cultural significance of their work.

For those wishing to explore Tunisian crafts beyond the markets, many cities offer **museums** and **cultural centers** that showcase the country's rich artistic heritage. The **Bardo Museum** in Tunis, for example, offers an in-depth look at Tunisia's **archaeological** and **artistic history**, with exhibits dedicated to ancient pottery, **Islamic calligraphy**, and **mosaics**. Visitors interested in purchasing **high-quality, handmade crafts** should also consider **visiting artisan cooperatives**, where goods are produced in a more formal setting and often come with certification of authenticity.

Tunisia's **art and craft scene** is a reflection of its cultural richness, its dedication to tradition, and its ongoing love for **handmade** goods. For any visitor, the experience of wandering through the **souks**, engaging with the artisans, and perhaps even taking home a piece of Tunisian craftsmanship, is one of the most rewarding parts of a trip to this beautiful and diverse country. The beauty and artistry of Tunisian **pottery**, **textiles**, **metalwork**, and **leather** are not only symbols of the country's heritage but also a way to bring home a piece of its soul.

CHAPTER 5: ADVENTURE, NATURE, & ACTIVITIES

Camel Rides, Hot Air Ballooning & Desert Camping

Tunisia, with its vast deserts and stunning landscapes, offers a wealth of **adventurous experiences** that allow visitors to immerse themselves in the beauty and majesty of the country's natural wonders. From the tranquil, sun-drenched **Sahara Desert** to the expansive **salt flats**, Tunisia offers an unparalleled opportunity for travelers seeking **camel safaris**, **hot air ballooning**, and **camping** experiences. These activities allow visitors to connect with the country's rich cultural heritage while enjoying unforgettable outdoor adventures in some of the most unique landscapes in the world.

Camel safaris are perhaps one of the most iconic and romantic ways to explore the Tunisian desert. The sight of a camel caravan silhouetted against the setting sun, the soft desert wind brushing your face, and the rhythmic sway of the camels beneath you creates an experience that feels both timeless and magical. The **Sahara Desert**, which stretches across southern Tunisia, is a popular location for these safaris, and numerous **tour operators** offer guided tours that range from a few hours to several days. These tours are ideal for those wanting to experience the desert's striking beauty in an authentic way, exploring the ever-changing dunes, visiting traditional **oasis towns**, and encountering local Bedouin culture. Many camel safari operators in southern Tunisia, particularly in places like **Douz** (often referred to as the "Gateway to the Sahara") or **Tozeur**, offer customizable packages that can be tailored to your interests and the time you have available. A typical day on a camel safari might begin in the early morning to catch the cooler hours, with travelers riding across the rolling dunes, taking short breaks to stretch and admire the vast desert landscape.

Costs for **camel safaris** can vary widely depending on the duration and the level of luxury. A half-day camel ride typically costs between **50-100 Tunisian Dinars** (around **$15-$30 USD**), while a full-day excursion may run from **150-250 Dinars** ($45-$75 USD). Multi-day safaris, including overnight camping in the desert under the stars, can cost significantly more, ranging from **300-600 Dinars** ($90-$180 USD), depending on whether meals, local guides, and accommodations are included. Some tours even provide **luxury options** with more comfortable arrangements such as **private tents**, **meals cooked over an open fire**, and **refreshments served in the desert**. When booking a camel safari, it is essential to check what's included in the price, as some packages include transportation, meals, and an expert guide, while others may not.

For those opting for longer camel treks or overnight stays, it's essential to **prepare** and **pack** adequately. Most tour operators will provide necessary items like **water**, **camel saddles**, and **basic camping equipment**. However, travelers should still consider bringing their own **sunscreen**, **protective clothing**, and **comfortable shoes** for walking. **Camel saddles** are typically padded, but if you're planning to ride for an extended period, it's a good idea to bring a **cushion** or **extra padding** for comfort. Keep in mind that the desert can be **extremely hot** during the day, with temperatures soaring to **40-45°C (104-113°F)** in the summer months, so you'll need to stay hydrated and protect yourself from the intense sun.

Hot air ballooning over the Tunisian desert or oasis towns is another **breathtaking** way to see the country's landscapes. The experience of floating silently over the desert, watching the sun rise over the vast dunes, and taking in the surrounding landscapes from above is both exhilarating and serene. The town of **Tozeur**, located near the Sahara Desert, is one of the most popular places to embark on a hot air ballooning adventure. From **Tozeur**, you can take off and soar above the desert landscape, the **Chott el Jerid salt flats**, and the surrounding **oasis towns**. Many tour operators in **Tozeur** offer hot air balloon flights, providing a unique bird's-eye view of the region. Depending on the wind conditions, flights usually take between **45 minutes to 1 hour**, and the experience includes a **pre-flight briefing**, **take-off**, and a **smooth landing** in a nearby field or desert area.

The cost of a **hot air balloon ride** varies but typically ranges from **250-600 Dinars** ($75-$180 USD) per person. This price generally includes the flight, a guide, and sometimes a post-flight celebration with a **glass of local juice** or **mint tea**. **Safety is paramount**, and most ballooning companies operate under strict regulations. Ballooning pilots are trained professionals, and balloons are regularly checked for **safety** and **maintenance**. However, visitors should still heed important advice: wear **comfortable clothes** and **sturdy shoes**, avoid heavy meals before flying, and bring a **camera** to capture the mesmerizing views. It's also worth noting that ballooning is highly dependent on weather conditions, so flights may be canceled due to **strong winds**, **rain**, or **low visibility**. Always check with the operator in advance for updates on weather conditions and flight availability.

For those looking to **experience the wilderness** in a more immersive way, **camping in the desert** or at the edge of an oasis is another unmissable experience. The desert landscape offers a striking beauty and an unmatched tranquility that is hard to find elsewhere. Camping in Tunisia allows visitors to truly disconnect from the modern world and embrace the peaceful, expansive emptiness of the desert. You can choose from **basic tented camps** (which might include simple **bedrolls** and **matting**) or more **luxurious desert camps** that offer larger tents with **real beds**, **private bathrooms**, and **meals prepared by local chefs**. Many camping tours in the **Sahara** also offer additional activities such as **stargazing**, **nighttime desert walks**, and **camel rides** to make the experience even more memorable.

Camping prices can vary significantly, with **basic campsites** costing between **40-80 Dinars ($12-$25 USD)** per person for a night, while more **luxurious desert camps** could range from **150-300 Dinars** ($45-$90 USD) or more per night. Most tours include meals, **refreshments**, and **water**, but it's always a good idea to double-check what's included when booking your stay. The best time to go camping is during the cooler months of **October to April**, as temperatures in the summer months can become **extremely hot**, especially in the afternoon. **Nighttime** in the desert is much cooler, with temperatures dropping rapidly, so it's advisable to bring **warm clothing**, even if you're visiting during the warmer months.

When camping in the desert, safety is a priority. The desert can be **isolated**, so always go with a **guided tour** led by experienced local guides who are familiar with the terrain and can provide assistance if needed. Guides will also ensure you have access to **water** and **supplies**, as well as maintain a **safe distance** from **wildlife**. It's important to follow all safety advice provided by the tour guides and to be aware of the desert's unique dangers, such as sudden **sandstorms** or **extreme temperature shifts**. Another tip for desert camping is to **respect local customs**, particularly around religious or cultural sites. Always ask for permission before taking photographs, especially of people or their homes.

The experiences of **camel safaris**, **hot air ballooning**, and **desert camping** offer a rare opportunity to **explore Tunisia's stunning natural beauty**, its desert landscapes, and its cultural heritage in a unique and unforgettable way. Whether you choose to ride across the shifting sands on the back of a camel, drift peacefully above the desert in a hot air balloon, or sleep beneath a canopy of stars, these activities provide visitors with a deeper understanding of Tunisia's rich **cultural traditions** and **untamed wilderness**. Regardless of the activity, **safety**, **preparation**, and **planning** are key to ensuring that your adventure is both safe and enjoyable, and the rewards—a sense of serenity, adventure, and connection to nature—are undoubtedly worth it.

Hiking Trails & Trekking

Hiking and trekking in Tunisia offer travelers a chance to explore the country's rugged interior, with dramatic landscapes, ancient olive groves, and remote mountain villages waiting to be discovered. Among the most notable regions for trekking are the **Atlas Mountains** and **Jebel Serj**, both of which offer diverse terrains and scenic views that are perfect for both beginner and experienced trekkers. These mountains provide an excellent opportunity to experience Tunisia's natural beauty, including its diverse flora, fauna, and rich cultural heritage.

The **Atlas Mountains** extend across several countries in North Africa, with the most prominent range in Tunisia being the **Tunisian Atlas**. This range stretches from the northwestern part of the country near **Tabarka**, to the south, where it converges with the vast expanses of the Sahara Desert. The **Atlas** is home to a variety of terrains, from rocky hills to steep cliffs and lush valleys, making it a paradise for those who enjoy exploring unspoiled nature.

One of the most popular trekking spots within this range is **Jebel Serj**, a peak located in the **Kasserine Governorate**, standing at about **1,500 meters (4,900 feet)** above sea level. The mountain is a haven for hikers looking for a mix of moderate climbs, picturesque landscapes, and access to remote villages.

The hiking experience in the Atlas Mountains is diverse and can cater to various skill levels. There are a number of well-maintained trails, ranging from easy, lowland walks to more demanding treks that take you through steep hills, valleys, and up rugged mountain peaks. One of the most popular trekking routes is the one leading to **Jebel Serj**. This trail is typically a **3 to 4-hour** hike that involves a moderate ascent, offering a satisfying challenge for most trekkers. Along the way, visitors will be able to see **olive groves**, **cypress forests**, and rocky outcrops that provide dramatic panoramic views of the surrounding countryside. In the spring, the hillsides are dotted with **wildflowers**, and in the cooler months, the snow-capped peaks of **Jebel Serj** offer a stunning contrast against the barren lands below.

The trek to **Jebel Serj** can be done as a **day hike**, but for those seeking to fully immerse themselves in the beauty of the region, a **multi-day trek** is also possible. Many guided tours are available that take visitors on longer treks, which include camping overnight in the mountain ranges or staying in **remote Berber villages** along the way. These longer treks usually last **2 to 4 days**, depending on the route chosen, and provide hikers the chance to experience local Berber culture and see traditional ways of life. Travelers can visit villages where stone houses are tucked into the mountainsides and interact with the friendly locals, many of whom still rely on agriculture and traditional farming techniques.

While **hiking** in the Atlas Mountains can be an incredibly rewarding experience, it's important to be prepared for the conditions. **Trekking in these mountains** can be physically demanding, especially if you are tackling the more challenging routes to **Jebel Serj**. The altitude can also make it harder for some visitors to adjust, so it's essential to acclimatize before attempting more strenuous hikes. The climate in the mountains varies significantly depending on the time of year. **Summers** can be quite hot, with temperatures reaching **30°C (86°F)** or higher, particularly in lower elevations, while **winters** can be cold, with temperatures occasionally dipping below **0°C (32°F)**, especially at higher altitudes. Therefore, **proper clothing** is essential. Lightweight, moisture-wicking layers for warmth and sun protection are crucial, and in colder months, bring an insulating jacket, gloves, and a hat. Always ensure that you have **sunscreen** and **sunglasses** to protect yourself from the sun, especially when trekking at higher altitudes.

The **cost** of hiking in Tunisia can vary, depending on whether you choose a **self-guided** trek or opt for a **guided tour**. For a **self-guided trek**, all you need to pay for is your transportation to the mountains, food, water, and any entrance fees to natural parks (if applicable). Local guides are usually not required for simpler, well-marked routes, but in more challenging areas or on longer treks, it's advisable to hire a guide. Guided treks typically cost between **150-400 Tunisian Dinars** ($45-$120 USD) per person per day, depending on the complexity of the trek, the length of the hike, and whether meals or equipment rentals are included. For example, a guided trek to **Jebel Serj** may cost **250-350 Dinars** ($75-$105 USD) for a one-day hike, while multi-day treks, which may include overnight camping or staying with local families, can cost upwards of **500 Dinars** ($150 USD) or more.

If you're planning on hiking in the Atlas Mountains or **Jebel Serj**, it's important to bring the right **hiking gear**. Most treks do not require highly specialized equipment, but some basics are necessary for a safe and enjoyable experience. Essential gear includes **sturdy hiking boots**, a **backpack**, **trekking poles** (optional but helpful for challenging terrain), a **water bottle** (refillable if possible), and a **first aid kit**. If you plan on camping, some companies offer **tent rentals** and provide necessary camping equipment, such as **sleeping bags** and **cooking gear**, for an additional cost. The rental of a full **camping set** usually costs around **30-50 Dinars** ($9-$15 USD) per day.

For **safety**, it is advisable to trek with a **guide** if you're unfamiliar with the terrain or hiking in the mountains for the first time. While the trails are generally well-marked, certain areas of the **Atlas Mountains** can be difficult to navigate without experience, and some routes may be **remote**, making it harder to find help in case of an emergency. It's also important to check the **weather forecast** before setting out. In the winter months, snow and ice can create dangerous conditions, particularly on higher trails. In the summer, **heatstroke** is a risk, especially during midday hikes. Always start your hikes early in the morning to avoid the midday heat and carry sufficient **water**—at least **2-3 liters** per person, especially if you plan to hike for several hours. **Wildlife** in the mountains is generally not dangerous, but it's still important to be cautious, particularly around **snakes** and **insects**.

Accommodation near the Atlas Mountains and Jebel Serj is available, ranging from budget **guesthouses** and **camping sites** to more comfortable **eco-lodges** and **hotels**. **Tozeur**, **Kairouan**, and **Tunis** are nearby cities that serve as good starting points for hiking trips. For trekkers planning a more immersive experience, many companies offer packages that include stays in **local Berber homes** or at **campsites** in the mountains. These options provide a unique cultural experience and offer the chance to sample local cuisine and learn about traditional mountain living.

For those looking to combine the experience of hiking with exploration of Tunisia's rich cultural and historical sites, the Atlas Mountains and **Jebel Serj** provide an excellent opportunity. Whether you choose to trek through peaceful olive groves, scale the heights of Jebel Serj for stunning views, or explore the small mountain villages nestled in the range, hiking in this part of Tunisia offers something for every outdoor enthusiast.

Ultimately, hiking and trekking in the Atlas Mountains and Jebel Serj is not just about the physical challenge; it's also about connecting with nature, experiencing the beauty of the desert-mountain interface, and appreciating the ancient traditions of the local people. With proper preparation and the right attitude, trekking in this region can be one of the most memorable experiences of your visit to Tunisia.

Diving and Snorkeling Hotspots

Diving and snorkeling in Tunisia offer travelers the chance to explore some of the most captivating underwater environments in the Mediterranean, from the vibrant coral reefs and underwater caves near **Djerba** to the rocky marine landscapes of **Tabarka**. The country's Mediterranean coastline is home to diverse marine life, clear waters, and a mix of coastal ecosystems that attract divers and snorkelers from around the world. Whether you're a seasoned diver or a first-time snorkeler, Tunisia's coastal areas provide an array of options for underwater adventures that are both accessible and breathtaking.

Djerba, an island off the southern coast of Tunisia, is one of the most popular destinations for **diving and snorkeling**. Its crystal-clear waters, calm seas, and diverse marine life make it ideal for both beginners and experienced divers. The island is known for its rich **marine biodiversity**, including colorful **coral gardens**, **sea turtles**, **groupers**, and a variety of **Mediterranean fish** species. Djerba's **underwater visibility** is generally excellent, often reaching depths of up to **30 meters** or more, which is perfect for exploring the many **shipwrecks**, underwater caves, and marine life habitats that surround the island. Many dive shops offer both **beginner courses** and

advanced certifications, along with guided dives to explore these amazing underwater landscapes.

If you're a beginner, **snorkeling** is a fantastic way to get a taste of the underwater world in Djerba. The island offers numerous shallow water sites, where you can swim over coral beds and see a wide variety of fish species without needing to go too deep. Snorkeling trips are usually organized from the island's beaches, and they typically last for about **1-2 hours**. **Rental equipment** for snorkeling is readily available, including **masks**, **snorkels**, and **fins**, which can be rented for around **15-30 Tunisian Dinars** ($5-$10 USD) per person for a half-day. There are also guided snorkeling tours that may include a boat trip to less accessible areas, providing an opportunity to explore isolated coves and hidden reefs. These guided tours usually cost between **50-100 Dinars** ($15-$30 USD) and may include refreshments and a local guide to help spot marine life.

For more experienced divers, **Djerba** offers a wealth of dive sites that cater to varying levels of expertise. Some of the most popular dive spots include the **Sidi Mahrez Reef**, a protected underwater area with rich marine life, and the **Zarzis Wreck**, which is perfect for wreck diving enthusiasts. The **Zenobia Wreck** near the island is also a popular destination for divers seeking to explore sunken ships. Dive trips in Djerba typically cost between **80-150 Dinars** ($25-$45 USD) for a single dive, and packages for multiple dives are also available at discounted rates. If you're looking for a more in-depth experience, many dive centers offer **PADI certification** courses, which range from the basic **Open Water Diver** course (usually lasting around 4-5 days and costing between **500-800 Dinars** or $150-$240 USD) to more advanced certifications, such as the **Advanced Open Water Diver** or **Rescue Diver**.

Tabarka, located along the northern coast of Tunisia, is another excellent destination for diving and snorkeling. Known for its dramatic rocky coastlines and the presence of the **Kuriat Islands**, Tabarka boasts some of the most beautiful and untouched dive sites in the Mediterranean. The waters off the coast of Tabarka are teeming with a variety of fish species, including **barracuda**, **grouper**, and **sea bass**, while the region is also famous for its rich coral gardens and underwater caves. Some of the more popular dive spots around Tabarka include **The Grotto of Tabarka**, a submerged cave system with incredible rock formations, and the **Kuriat Islands**, which offer a mix of deep-water diving and shallow areas ideal for snorkeling.

Diving in Tabarka is a bit different from Djerba due to the **stronger currents** in the area, making it a more challenging location for beginners. However, it's a paradise for **advanced divers** and those seeking an authentic Mediterranean diving experience. **Scuba diving trips** in Tabarka typically cost around **100-150 Dinars** ($30-$45 USD) for a single dive, and diving centers often offer packages for multiple dives, which are more affordable. For beginners, **snorkeling trips** are also available at **Kuriat Islands** and other accessible sites along the coast, with prices ranging from **40-70 Dinars** ($12-$20 USD) for a guided experience. **Rental equipment** for snorkeling is available at dive shops and beach resorts, with prices similar to those found in Djerba.

The Mediterranean coast of Tunisia also offers opportunities for **boat trips** that combine both **snorkeling and diving**, particularly in the **Kuriat Islands** area, which is known for its shallow waters, vibrant coral, and diverse fish life. Most boat trips last for about **half a day**, and prices for combined activities generally start around **60-100 Dinars** ($18-$30 USD). Many operators provide everything you need, including **transportation, snorkeling gear**, and **onboard refreshments**.

If you're planning to go diving or snorkeling in Tunisia, it's essential to consider safety. While the Mediterranean waters are generally calm, especially in the summer months, certain areas can have strong currents, particularly around **Tabarka**. It's important to check with dive operators about the conditions on the day of your dive and ensure you have a guide if you're not familiar with the area. For those going **scuba diving**, ensure that you're physically fit and have the necessary certifications if you plan to dive deeper than **18 meters (60 feet)**. If you're a beginner, it's advisable to stick to the shallower sites where you can easily access the surface if needed. Always dive with a **buddy**, and never exceed your level of experience or comfort.

When renting equipment, ensure that the **mask, snorkel**, and **fins** fit properly, as ill-fitting gear can make the experience uncomfortable and hinder your enjoyment. It's also a good idea to carry a **waterproof bag** for your personal belongings, as many dive shops and resorts provide you with storage lockers, but some trips may involve boat rides to more remote sites where such amenities may not be available.

For **divers** seeking more advanced experiences, there are also opportunities to try out **wreck diving** and **cave diving**, particularly near **Djerba** and **Tabarka**, where there are a number of submerged historical sites to explore. These types of dives require more experience and specialized equipment, and divers are advised to book through professional operators who specialize in these types of dives.

Tunisia's Mediterranean coast is an incredible destination for those interested in **diving and snorkeling**. With its clear waters, diverse marine life, and access to both beginner-friendly and challenging dive sites, it offers experiences for all levels. Whether you're looking to explore the vibrant underwater world off the coast of **Djerba**, the dramatic underwater landscapes of **Tabarka**, or the peaceful waters of **the Kuriat Islands**, Tunisia provides a stunning setting for unforgettable marine adventures. With the right preparation, equipment, and professional guidance, diving and snorkeling in Tunisia can be an enriching and exhilarating experience, offering insights into one of the most beautiful and diverse marine ecosystems in the Mediterranean.

Sustainable Tourism & Wildlife Encounters

Sustainable travel is becoming an increasingly important part of exploring destinations that are both ecologically sensitive and culturally rich. In Tunisia, a country blessed with diverse landscapes, ancient ruins, and stunning natural reserves, the idea of **eco-tourism** has gained traction, with more visitors seeking out sustainable travel options and wildlife experiences that respect the environment while allowing travelers to witness the beauty of nature. The country's vast deserts, rugged mountain ranges, and coastal areas are home to a rich variety of wildlife, including endangered species, migratory birds, and marine life, making Tunisia an ideal destination for sustainable wildlife watching.

One of the best places to experience **sustainable travel** and **wildlife watching** is **Djerba Island**, known for its laid-back atmosphere and commitment to preserving its natural environment. Djerba is an excellent location for ecotourism, with **wildlife reserves** and conservation projects aimed at protecting the island's unique fauna and flora. One such project is the **Djerba Island Flamingo Reserve**, located near the **Oued El Kebir** wetlands. The reserve is a prime location for bird watching, where visitors can spot large flocks of **flamingos, herons, waders**, and other migratory birds, particularly between **March and October**, when the wetlands are alive with migratory species. To ensure minimal disturbance to wildlife, visitors are encouraged to take guided tours that follow strict environmental protocols and avoid disrupting the natural habitat. **Bird watching tours** here typically cost between **30-50 Dinars** ($10-$15 USD) for a half-day guided tour, with additional charges for transportation if required.

Further south, **Tozeur**, a town known for its proximity to the **Chott El Jerid salt flats**, also serves as a hub for **eco-tourism** and **wildlife watching**. This region is part of the **Tunisian Sahara Desert**, which is home to a variety of resilient desert wildlife. Although the region is known for its arid landscapes, it also boasts some incredible conservation efforts aimed at protecting desert-adapted species such as the **Barbary sheep**, **wild gazelles**, and various species of **lizards** and **birds of prey**. For wildlife enthusiasts, **camel treks** through the **Sahara** provide opportunities to experience the desert's ecosystem firsthand. These camel treks are usually conducted in small groups, reducing the environmental footprint of the tours and ensuring that the ecosystem remains intact. Camel trek tours in **Tozeur** generally range from **100-250 Dinars** ($30-$75 USD) per person, depending on the length of the trek and whether it includes overnight stays in desert camps. Many of these tours focus on sustainable practices, like using **local guides**, traveling with **minimal environmental impact**, and ensuring wildlife encounters are both respectful and educational.

The **Kuriat Islands** off the coast of **Tabarka** in northern Tunisia also represent a sustainable tourism destination. These islands are home to a variety of bird species, including migratory seabirds and native species that rely on the islands for nesting and rest. The islands are a protected

marine and bird sanctuary, and eco-tourism initiatives focus on educating visitors about the importance of conservation in preserving the delicate ecosystems of the islands. **Eco-friendly boat tours** to the Kuriat Islands are available from **Tabarka**. These tours are designed to have minimal impact on the environment, and travelers are advised to take only guided tours to ensure that they do not disrupt the natural habitats of the birds and marine life. The cost for a boat tour to the Kuriat Islands ranges from **50-100 Dinars** ($15-$30 USD), depending on the type of tour and duration.

For those looking to explore more of Tunisia's **wildlife reserves**, the **Ichkeul National Park**, a UNESCO World Heritage site, is one of the most important and biodiverse regions in the country. Located in the north, near the town of **Bizerte**, the park is home to the **Ichkeul Lake**, a vital wetland that attracts thousands of **migratory birds** every year. The park is a prime spot for bird watchers, particularly in winter when species like **white storks**, **ducks**, and **geese** stop here to rest during their migrations. The park's biodiversity also includes **wild boars**, **foxes**, and various types of **reptiles**. The park has implemented various eco-tourism initiatives, such as **sustainable hiking trails**, guided eco-tours, and educational programs about the importance of wetland conservation. Entrance to the park typically costs around **5-10 Dinars** ($1.50-$3 USD), with additional costs for guided tours. If you're interested in a more immersive experience, **camping** is also available within the park, but visitors must bring their own equipment, as camping is strictly regulated to maintain the integrity of the park.

In addition to these natural areas, Tunisia's commitment to **eco-tourism** is seen in its efforts to protect its coastal regions, particularly along the **Mediterranean coast**. Marine life conservation projects focus on preserving endangered species such as **sea turtles**, **dolphins**, and **monk seals**, which are occasionally spotted in coastal waters, particularly around **Sidi Bou Said** and **Hammamet**. **Snorkeling tours** are available in these areas, offering an opportunity to observe the marine life in its natural habitat while also promoting the importance of sustainable marine tourism. **Snorkeling trips** typically cost around **30-60 Dinars** ($9-$18 USD), and operators generally follow eco-friendly practices, such as using **non-toxic sunscreen** and encouraging responsible behavior like avoiding contact with coral reefs or disturbing marine species.

Visitors interested in **sustainable travel** in Tunisia should also consider the ecological practices of the accommodations they choose. Many hotels and resorts along Tunisia's coast are starting to adopt green practices, from **solar-powered energy** and **water conservation** systems to organic gardens and waste recycling programs. In areas like **Hammamet** and **Sousse**, some eco-resorts offer all-inclusive stays with an emphasis on supporting local economies and promoting environmental responsibility.

When engaging in wildlife watching or sustainable travel activities, it is crucial for visitors to adhere to some basic **safety and ethical guidelines** to ensure that their activities do not negatively impact the environment. For instance, whether trekking in the mountains or visiting wildlife reserves, it is vital to follow **leave-no-trace** principles, which include packing out all trash, avoiding unnecessary noise that could disturb wildlife, and staying on designated trails. When participating in wildlife watching, always choose to travel with operators who follow ethical guidelines, such as ensuring that wildlife is viewed from a safe distance and not approached too closely. Additionally, avoid touching or feeding wild animals, as this can alter their natural behavior and endanger their health.

For those seeking more adventurous eco-tourism experiences, there are **nature conservation programs** and **volunteer opportunities** in Tunisia, where you can contribute directly to preserving the country's natural resources. Programs often focus on activities like **tree planting, wildlife monitoring**, and **coastal clean-up efforts**. Many of these projects are organized by local NGOs or conservation organizations, and participants can get involved for a week or more. These experiences are not only fulfilling but also offer travelers a deeper connection to the landscape they're exploring.

The cost for such conservation activities varies depending on the organization and the type of program. Many programs include basic accommodations, meals, and equipment, with prices ranging from **200-500 Dinars** ($60-$150 USD) for a week-long experience. These programs are ideal for those looking to make a positive impact while traveling, as they allow visitors to contribute directly to local conservation efforts.

Tunisia offers a variety of sustainable travel and wildlife-watching opportunities for those who wish to connect with nature in a responsible and meaningful way. From exploring the **vast deserts of Tozeur** to discovering the lush, biodiverse ecosystems of **Ichkeul National Park**, travelers can experience some of the most beautiful natural landscapes in the Mediterranean while supporting efforts to protect them. By choosing responsible travel options and adhering to sustainable tourism practices, visitors can enjoy Tunisia's natural wonders without leaving a negative footprint, making their travels both rewarding and environmentally conscious.

CHAPTER 6: ACCOMMODATION

Hotels and Resorts

Tunisia offers a wide range of hotels and resorts catering to every type of traveler, from luxury seekers to budget-conscious explorers. Whether you're visiting bustling cities like Tunis, enjoying the serene beaches of Djerba, or exploring the historic and cultural sights of the inland towns, there are ample accommodation options designed to provide comfort, convenience, and authentic Tunisian hospitality. Each destination in Tunisia offers its own unique experience, and the accommodation choices reflect the diversity of the country's attractions and landscapes.

In **Tunis**, the capital city, you'll find a variety of **hotels** that blend modern amenities with the charm of the old city. One standout is the **Sheraton Tunis Hotel**, located in the heart of the city on **Avenue Mohamed V**. This five-star hotel is just a short drive from the famous **Medina of Tunis** and the **Bardo Museum**, making it an ideal base for those wishing to explore the historical side of the capital. The hotel features spacious rooms with a mix of modern design and traditional Tunisian touches, a large outdoor pool, and a well-equipped fitness center. There are also several dining options, including international and local cuisine. The Sheraton is known for its luxurious service, and the cost for a night here typically ranges from **150-250 Dinars**

($45-$80 USD), depending on the season and room type. The **check-in time** is generally at **3:00 PM**, while **check-out** is by **12:00 PM**. To reach the hotel, taxis and private transfers are readily available from **Tunis-Carthage International Airport**, which is about **10 kilometers (6 miles)** away, taking around **20-30 minutes**.

For those seeking a more boutique and authentic experience in **Tunis**, the **Dar El Jeld Hotel** offers a charming stay in a traditional Tunisian riad-style building, located near the historic Medina. This luxury boutique hotel is a former palace, offering an intimate, stylish atmosphere with modern amenities blended with classic design elements. It is perfectly situated for those interested in exploring the **Medina's narrow streets**, **souks**, and ancient landmarks, such as the **Zitouna Mosque**. The hotel features an on-site restaurant serving Tunisian delicacies and a rooftop terrace with stunning views of the city. Room rates here are generally in the range of **120-180 Dinars** ($35-$55 USD) per night. Check-in and check-out times are similar, with check-in at **2:00 PM** and check-out at **12:00 PM**. The hotel is about **15-20 minutes** from the airport, depending on traffic.

For a beachside getaway, **Djerba Island** is a popular destination, particularly for those seeking resorts that blend relaxation with traditional Tunisian culture. One of the most luxurious resorts on the island is the **Hasdrubal Thalassa & Spa Djerba**, located in **Midoun**, near the island's famous sandy beaches. This five-star resort offers an all-inclusive experience, with an expansive thalassotherapy spa, multiple outdoor pools, a private beach area, and various sports activities, including tennis and water sports. The resort's architecture is inspired by the traditional Djerban style, with whitewashed walls and blue accents, creating a peaceful and luxurious atmosphere. Guests can enjoy both international and Mediterranean cuisine at the resort's various restaurants. Prices at this resort typically range from **250-400 Dinars** ($75-$120 USD) per night, and the check-in time is **2:00 PM**, with check-out at **12:00 PM**. The resort is located about **30 minutes** from **Djerba-Zarzis International Airport**.

Another popular choice in Djerba is the **Hotel Radisson Blu Palace Resort & Thalasso**, located in the coastal town of **Yasmine**. This hotel is known for its extensive wellness offerings, with an award-winning thalasso spa, fitness center, and stunning beachfront views. It's a great spot for couples or families looking for both relaxation and adventure. Guests can enjoy water activities, including **windsurfing** and **jet skiing**, or simply relax by one of the resort's pools or on the beach. The average cost for a night at the Radisson Blu is between **150-250 Dinars** ($45-$80 USD), depending on the room and season. This hotel is a bit closer to the **Djerba International Airport**, about **20-25 minutes** by taxi or private transport.

In the **Sousse** region, the **Mövenpick Resort & Marine Spa Sousse** is an excellent choice for those seeking a luxurious stay near the beach and the city's main attractions. This upscale hotel is located on the coast, just a short distance from the historic **Medina of Sousse**, **Ribat**, and the **Great Mosque**. The hotel offers stylish rooms with ocean views, a large outdoor pool, a private beach, and an extensive **spa and wellness center**. Guests can enjoy international cuisine, as well as traditional Tunisian dishes, in several on-site restaurants. The cost for a stay here generally ranges from **150-300 Dinars** ($45-$90 USD) per night, with check-in at **3:00 PM** and check-out at **12:00 PM**. The hotel is located about **20 minutes** from **Monastir Habib Bourguiba International Airport**, making it easy to access from the airport via taxi.

For those looking to experience a more budget-friendly yet charming accommodation, **El Kantaoui** is a coastal town near **Sousse** offering several mid-range hotels. The **El Mouradi Hotel** is a popular option, offering a great balance of value and amenities. Located near the **Port El Kantaoui Marina**, this hotel offers easy access to the marina's shops, restaurants, and watersports activities, as well as the **Acqua Palace Water Park**. The hotel features a pool, a beach area, and comfortable rooms with modern amenities. Prices at **El Mouradi Hotel** typically start at **80-120 Dinars** ($25-$40 USD) per night. The hotel is about **30 minutes** from **Monastir Airport**, and it's well-connected by taxi.

For those wishing to explore the inland, **Kairouan**, a UNESCO World Heritage site, is a must-visit for history enthusiasts. The **Riadh Palms Hotel**, located just outside the city, offers a peaceful and relaxing atmosphere with traditional Tunisian charm. Its proximity to the historical center makes it ideal for exploring the **Great Mosque of Kairouan**, **Aghlabid Basins**, and **Medina**, all within walking distance. The hotel offers spacious rooms, a pool, and an on-site restaurant serving both local and international cuisine. Room rates at the Riadh Palms are typically **60-100 Dinars** ($20-$30 USD) per night. This hotel provides a great opportunity to stay close to the heart of Kairouan's historic attractions, while also offering a comfortable, peaceful retreat. It's located about **5-10 minutes** from the city center by taxi.

Tunisia's **beach resorts** are undoubtedly some of the most sought-after places for relaxation, and many offer all-inclusive packages, making them excellent options for those looking to unwind. Resorts like **Iberostar Averroes Hotel** in **Hammamet** also provide travelers with luxurious beachfront access and a comprehensive selection of activities, including tennis, golf, and water sports. With prices generally ranging from **120-250 Dinars** ($35-$75 USD) per night, these all-inclusive resorts offer great value, especially for families or groups.

No matter where you choose to stay, Tunisia's hotels and resorts offer something for every type of traveler, whether you're seeking a luxury stay with spa treatments and fine dining or a budget-friendly spot near Tunisia's famous landmarks. The most important things to keep in mind when booking your accommodation include **location**, **amenities**, and **seasonality**, as prices can fluctuate greatly depending on the time of year, with summer months typically being more expensive. It's always advisable to check the hotel's cancellation policy and ensure that the property you choose aligns with your preferences for a seamless and enjoyable stay.

Unique & Alternative Stays

While many visitors gravitate toward conventional hotels and resorts, those looking for a unique and immersive experience will find that Tunisia offers a wide range of **alternative accommodations** that offer something different. These unique stays allow travelers to connect with Tunisia's culture, history, and natural beauty in an unforgettable way.

For those seeking a **traditional and authentic Tunisian experience**, staying in a **riad** (a traditional house with a central courtyard) is a fantastic option. In the heart of **Tunis**, the **Dar Ben Gacem** is a perfect example of this type of accommodation. Located in the **Medina of Tunis**, this 17th-century house has been beautifully restored to combine traditional architecture with modern comforts. Staying here is like stepping into another era—rooms are adorned with intricate Tunisian tiles, wooden beams, and vintage furniture. The location is ideal for exploring the Medina, with its winding alleys, ancient mosques, and bustling souks just a short walk away. The riad offers a cozy courtyard, perfect for enjoying a traditional Tunisian breakfast, and provides a quiet retreat from the noise of the city. Prices at **Dar Ben Gacem** typically range from **90-150 Dinars** ($30-$50 USD) per night for a standard room, with **check-in** available from **2:00 PM** and **check-out** by **12:00 PM**. The riad is about **20-25 minutes** from **Tunis-Carthage International Airport** by taxi or private transport.

If you're heading to the **Sahara Desert** and want to experience the vastness of the dunes in a truly unique way, consider staying in a **desert camp**. One of the best known is **Ksar Ghilane**, an oasis located in the southern part of Tunisia, close to the Libyan border. This desert camp offers a blend of adventure and luxury, where visitors can spend the night in traditional **Berber tents** equipped with comfortable bedding and modern amenities like electricity and air conditioning. **Ksar Ghilane** is one of the most famous oases in Tunisia, known for its hot springs and its proximity to **Chott El Jerid**, the largest salt flat in the country. Visitors can also embark on camel treks or enjoy **star-gazing** in the clear desert sky. The camp offers traditional meals served under the stars, allowing guests to enjoy local dishes while surrounded by the stunning desert landscape. Prices for a stay at **Ksar Ghilane Desert Camp** generally start from **150-250 Dinars** ($50-$80 USD) per person per night, including meals and excursions. The **check-in time** is usually **3:00 PM**, and **check-out** is at **12:00 PM**. To get there, travelers will typically need to fly to **Tozeur-Nefta Airport** and then take a **4-5 hour drive** to the camp, with most tours offering transport services.

For those who enjoy staying in **eco-friendly** accommodations, the **Eco-Lodge Ksar Ouled Soltane** in the **Tozeur** region offers a unique blend of sustainability and cultural immersion. This eco-lodge is set in a traditional **Berber village**, and the buildings are constructed from **adobe and clay**, materials that help regulate the temperature in the extreme heat of the desert. The lodge offers simple, yet comfortable rooms and an open-air restaurant serving traditional **Tunisian** food made from local ingredients. Guests can enjoy **guided tours** to nearby attractions, such as the **Chott El Jerid salt flats** and the famous **Tataouine** village, which inspired the set design for **Star Wars**. The lodge also organizes **camel rides** and offers **cultural workshops** on traditional Berber crafts and customs. A night's stay at **Ksar Ouled Soltane** costs around **100-150 Dinars** ($35-$50 USD), with **check-in** typically available from **2:00 PM** and **check-out** at **12:00 PM**. The lodge is accessible by taxi from **Tozeur-Nefta Airport**, which is approximately **30 minutes** away.

In the more **remote** parts of Tunisia, specifically the **Matmata** region, visitors can experience the extraordinary opportunity to stay in a **troglodyte house**, which are homes built into the earth. These homes are cool in the summer and warm in the winter, and they offer a truly unique living experience. The **Hotel Troglodyte Matmata** offers guests the chance to stay in these fascinating underground homes, and it's located near the famous **Matmata** village, known for its distinctive architecture. The rooms in the hotel are carved into the hillsides, with traditional Berber furnishings and hand-painted walls. The hotel's location makes it an excellent choice for those exploring the **Djerba** region or visiting the nearby **Douz** desert, as it is well-positioned for cultural tours and camel treks. The cost of staying at **Hotel Troglodyte Matmata** is approximately **80-120 Dinars** ($25-$40 USD) per night. **Check-in** is typically **2:00 PM**, with **check-out** at **12:00 PM**. To reach the hotel, travelers can fly into **Tozeur-Nefta Airport**, then take a **1.5-2 hour taxi ride** to the village of Matmata.

For those who are looking for a more luxurious and unconventional experience, the **Palace El Menzah** in **Tunis** offers a stay that blends history with opulence. This palatial hotel is housed in a **19th-century mansion**, and it features rooms that retain their historical charm while offering modern amenities. The hotel is located near several key attractions, including the **Carthage ruins**, the **Roman Theater**, and the **Bardo Museum**, making it an ideal choice for visitors who want to explore Tunis's rich history. The **Palace El Menzah** features beautiful **gardens**, a **swimming pool**, a **spa**, and **gourmet restaurants**. This is a more upscale accommodation, with room rates typically ranging from **250-400 Dinars** ($80-$120 USD) per night, depending on the room and season. The check-in time is **3:00 PM**, and check-out is at **12:00 PM**. To reach the hotel, it is about **20-30 minutes** by taxi from **Tunis-Carthage International Airport**.

For those seeking a more laid-back and rustic experience, staying in a **charming guesthouse** or **homestay** in a traditional Tunisian village offers a great way to immerse yourself in local culture. In the town of **Kairouan**, known for its significant religious history, the **Dar Al Andalus** guesthouse provides visitors with an authentic and intimate experience. Located in the heart of the **Medina**, this guesthouse features traditional architecture with modern touches. Guests can enjoy home-cooked Tunisian meals prepared with locally sourced ingredients and experience the warmth of Tunisian hospitality. Rates for a stay here usually begin at around **60-100 Dinars** ($20-$30 USD) per night, and the check-in time is generally **2:00 PM**, with check-out by **12:00 PM**. Kairouan is well-connected to other major Tunisian cities by both bus and train, and the guesthouse is just a short walk from the city's historical monuments, such as the **Great Mosque of Kairouan** and the **Aghlabid Basins**.

Whether you are staying in a **traditional riad** in **Tunis**, a **desert camp** in the Sahara, or a **troglodyte house** in **Matmata**, Tunisia offers a range of **unique accommodations** that provide travelers with the opportunity to engage with the country's rich culture and history. From **eco-lodges** to **historical palaces**, these alternative stays allow you to experience Tunisia in ways that go beyond the typical hotel experience. Prices vary depending on the location and type of accommodation, but many offer excellent value for the level of uniqueness and cultural immersion they provide. Whatever your budget or interests, these unique accommodations promise to make your stay in Tunisia a memorable one.

CHAPTER 7: PRACTICAL TIPS

Getting Around Tunisia: Transport Tips

Getting around Tunisia is relatively straightforward, and there are various transport options catering to different preferences and budgets. Whether you're exploring the historic streets of Tunis, venturing into the Sahara Desert, or relaxing along the Mediterranean coast, understanding how to navigate the country's transport systems can enhance your experience. The country has a solid network of public transport, taxis, and car rental services that will help you get from one destination to another efficiently, though some services are better suited to tourists than others.

Public transport in Tunisia includes buses, trains, and the **metro** system in Tunis. It is an affordable and efficient way to travel within cities, but may not be as convenient for exploring remote areas or reaching smaller towns. The **Tunis Metro** is especially handy for getting around in **Tunis** itself, offering an easy way to access popular areas such as **Carthage**, **La Marsa**, and **Belvédère Park**. The **Tunis Metro** operates from **5:30 AM** to **11:00 PM**, with trains running approximately every **15-20 minutes** during peak hours. The fare is inexpensive, with tickets typically costing around **1-1.5 Dinars** ($0.30-$0.50 USD) per ride, though day passes can be a good option for tourists planning to use the metro multiple times throughout the day. You can buy tickets directly from the ticket booth or from automated machines available at metro stations. The **Tunis Metro** connects with other public transport systems, such as the **Tunis tram**, which also serves several areas in the city.

For traveling **between cities**, **trains** offer a comfortable, affordable, and scenic way to explore Tunisia's landscapes. The national railway service, **SNCFT (Société Nationale des Chemins de Fer Tunisiens)**, operates a wide network of trains connecting major cities like **Tunis**, **Sousse**, **Monastir**, **Mahdia**, **Sfax**, and **Gabès**. Trains are well-maintained and air-conditioned, making them a popular choice during the hot summer months. The train station in **Tunis** is located at **Gare de Tunis** on **Avenue de la République**, a short walk from the **Medina** and the city's central business district. You can easily buy tickets at the station or online through the SNCFT website or mobile app. Train fares vary depending on the distance and class, but prices are generally around **5-30 Dinars** ($2-$10 USD) for a one-way trip. **First-class** tickets cost more, typically between **15-30 Dinars**, while **second-class** tickets are cheaper, ranging from **5-15 Dinars**. Trains run throughout the day, with frequent services between major cities. **SNCFT trains** generally operate between **6:00 AM** and **9:00 PM**, with timetables available online or at the station.

For those who prefer more **personalized** transportation, **taxis** are widely available and can be flagged down on the street or booked in advance through various services. The **white taxis** are the most common and are metered, with a base fare starting at about **1-2 Dinars** ($0.30-$0.60 USD), depending on the city. Taxis in **Tunis** charge about **1 Dinar** for the first kilometer, and around **1 Dinar** for every additional **500 meters**. For longer distances or rides outside city limits, drivers will usually agree on a fixed fare. Be sure to ask the driver to use the meter or agree on the price before starting the ride. In **Tunis**, there are also **collective taxis**, which operate on set routes and pick up passengers along the way, making them a slightly cheaper option, especially for shorter trips within the city. These taxis typically charge **2-4 Dinars** ($0.70-$1.30 USD) depending on the distance and destination.

In addition to regular taxis, you can also opt for private **ride-hailing services** similar to Uber, such as **Bolt** and **Yassir**, which are available in major cities like **Tunis** and **Sousse**. Using these services is particularly convenient if you want to avoid negotiating fares and prefer to have the price calculated in advance. **Bolt** operates throughout Tunisia and allows users to book rides via their mobile app. Prices are typically slightly higher than regular taxis, but the service is more reliable, and the convenience of cashless payments is a plus. For instance, a ride from **Tunis-Carthage International Airport** to downtown **Tunis** might cost around **15-25 Dinars** ($5-$8 USD), depending on traffic and the time of day.

For those seeking more **adventurous** and **flexible options**, **car rentals** provide the freedom to explore Tunisia at your own pace. Major international car rental companies like **Avis**, **Europcar**, and **Hertz** operate in **Tunis-Carthage International Airport**, as well as in major cities like

Sousse, **Djerba**, and **Sfax**. Rental offices are generally located within the airport terminals or in nearby locations in the city. You can book a car rental in advance through their websites or through various travel booking platforms. Prices typically start at around **80-120 Dinars** ($25-$40 USD) per day for an economy car, and may go higher depending on the type of car and rental duration. **Compact cars** are the most common rental options and are ideal for navigating narrow streets in Tunisia's cities, while **4x4 vehicles** are highly recommended for exploring the desert or remote regions like **Chott El Jerid** and **Ksar Ghilane**. When renting a car, it's essential to have a **valid international driver's license**, as well as **insurance** to cover any potential accidents. Some rental companies offer **GPS** units, but many visitors find using a smartphone map app (such as Google Maps) sufficient for most trips.

Although Tunisia's **road network** is generally good, **driving in Tunis** can be chaotic, especially in the **Medina** area where streets are narrow, and traffic is dense. Driving outside major cities is easier, though some rural roads might be poorly marked, so having a GPS or a local guide is helpful. It's important to note that **seat belts** are required by law, and **traffic lights** in certain areas may not always be followed, so exercising caution while driving is advised.

If you prefer not to rent a car but want to explore more remote areas, **private tours** can also be a good option. Many travel agencies in Tunisia offer tailored tours, whether for a day trip to **Carthage** or a multi-day adventure through the desert. These tours can be booked in advance or at travel agencies in major cities. Prices for a day tour typically range from **150-300 Dinars** ($50-$100 USD) per person, including transportation, a guide, and sometimes meals.

For a truly **local experience**, **shared minibuses** or **louages** (shared taxis) are popular for traveling between towns. These vehicles are an affordable way to get between destinations, though they can be cramped and less comfortable than private taxis. Louages operate on set routes, with passengers sharing the ride. They usually depart when they are full and are much cheaper than private taxis, with fares typically ranging from **10-30 Dinars** ($3-$10 USD) for longer routes.

Getting around Tunisia offers a variety of options depending on your comfort level, budget, and travel needs. **Public transportation** like buses and the **metro** provide an affordable and reliable way to travel within cities, while taxis and ride-hailing services offer more flexibility for getting around. For those looking to venture beyond the cities or explore Tunisia's unique landscapes, **car rentals** and **private tours** provide an excellent way to see the country at your own pace. With the right preparation and a bit of local know-how, navigating Tunisia is easy, and you can enjoy all that this fascinating country has to offer.

Souvenirs & Authentic Finds to Bring Home

Shopping in Tunisia is an essential part of the travel experience, offering visitors the chance to take home a variety of unique, culturally rich souvenirs. From handcrafted textiles and intricate pottery to spices and fine jewelry, Tunisia's markets (souks) are brimming with treasures that reflect the country's deep history, traditions, and craftsmanship. Whether you're strolling through the winding alleys of the Medina in Tunis or exploring the vibrant souks of Sousse, there are plenty of items that will make your trip memorable long after you've returned home.

One of the most popular and iconic souvenirs in Tunisia is **ceramic pottery**. Tunisia's pottery is renowned for its bright colors and intricate designs, often featuring traditional patterns and motifs. **Nabeul**, a town located about 60 kilometers east of Tunis, is the heart of ceramic production in the country. The **Nabeul Pottery Souk**, located in the heart of the town, is where you can find a wide variety of handcrafted plates, bowls, vases, and decorative tiles. Prices for small items like plates or mugs start at **5-15 Dinars** ($1.50-$5 USD), while larger pieces, such as vases or ornate wall hangings, can range from **25-50 Dinars** ($8-$17 USD), depending on size and complexity. These vibrant pieces are ideal for bringing home a piece of Tunisia's artistic heritage.

Another must-buy in Tunisia is **traditional carpets and rugs**. These are crafted by skilled artisans using a variety of techniques passed down through generations. The city of **Kairouan**, one of Tunisia's oldest cities, is famous for its handwoven rugs, known for their durability and beauty. The **Kairouan Carpet Souk** offers an array of choices, from small prayer rugs to large decorative pieces. Expect to pay anywhere from **50 Dinars** ($16 USD) for a small, simple rug, up to **500 Dinars** ($170 USD) or more for an intricate, high-quality carpet. When shopping for carpets, it's important to inspect the weaving and the material used—wool is common, but some rugs are made of silk, which can be more expensive. The best way to ensure you're getting a fair price is to haggle, as bargaining is a common practice in Tunisian markets.

Tunisian **jewelry** is another popular souvenir, particularly pieces made from **silver** and **semi-precious stones** like **amber**, **coral**, and **turquoise**. **Silversmiths** in cities such as **Tunis**, **Sousse**, and **Mednine** create exquisite rings, bracelets, necklaces, and earrings. A simple silver pendant can cost **10-20 Dinars** ($3-$6 USD), while larger, more elaborate pieces, such as silver bracelets or rings set with gemstones, can be priced between **30-150 Dinars** ($10-$50 USD), depending on the craftsmanship and materials used. The **Medina of Tunis** is home to numerous jewelry shops, where you'll find unique pieces that reflect Tunisia's Arab and Berber heritage. If you're in **Sousse**, head to the **Medina souk** or the **Haroun Souk**, where vendors display an impressive selection of silver jewelry.

For those interested in **traditional clothing**, Tunisia offers a variety of handmade textiles. The **Jubba**, a traditional long cloak worn by men, and the **Kaftan**, a flowing dress often worn by women, are both popular souvenirs. You can find these garments in **Tunis** or **Sousse**, often crafted from high-quality wool or silk and adorned with intricate embroidery. Prices for these pieces can vary, with a simple **Jubba** costing between **50-100 Dinars** ($16-$33 USD) and a more elaborate **Kaftan** ranging from **100-300 Dinars** ($33-$100 USD). These garments often come in a variety of colors and patterns, and they make perfect souvenirs for those seeking something authentically Tunisian.

Tunisian spices also make for great souvenirs, as they reflect the rich culinary traditions of the country. **Harissa**, a spicy chili paste, is one of the most famous products in Tunisia and can be found at markets throughout the country. The **Medina of Tunis** is an excellent place to find harissa, alongside other local spices such as **cumin**, **coriander**, **caraway**, and **saffron**. You can purchase small packets or larger jars of spices for as little as **2-5 Dinars** ($0.70-$1.70 USD) for a packet, with premium saffron costing more at around **50-100 Dinars** ($17-$33 USD) for a small container. Spices are often sold in colorful bags or jars, making them easy to transport back home.

If you're looking for something more decorative, **Tunisian leather** products are both practical and beautiful. Tunisia has a long history of leather production, with **Sfax** and **Tunis** being the centers of the industry. **Leather bags**, **wallets**, **belts**, and **shoes** can be found in markets like the **Medina of Tunis** and the **Medina of Sfax**, where skilled artisans create high-quality products from locally sourced leather. A handmade leather wallet can cost around **20-40 Dinars** ($6-$13 USD), while leather bags or shoes are priced between **40-150 Dinars** ($13-$50 USD), depending on size and craftsmanship. These items make for both stylish and functional souvenirs and are sure to last for years.

For art lovers, Tunisia's **traditional paintings** and **handicrafts** are great mementos of your trip. Tunisia has a thriving arts scene, and many local artists showcase their work in galleries and souks. You can find **canvas paintings** featuring landscapes, portraits, and traditional Tunisian scenes, especially in areas like **Tunis, Sousse**, and **Djerba**. Prices for small paintings start at around **50 Dinars** ($16 USD), while larger or more elaborate pieces can reach **200-400 Dinars** ($67-$133 USD), depending on the artist and the complexity of the piece. Art lovers should also keep an eye out for **Berber jewelry**, **metalwork**, and **wooden carvings**, all of which are often displayed alongside paintings in these markets.

If you're after a unique experience, **Tunisian perfumes** offer something special. Tunisia is known for producing high-quality, natural perfumes, especially in the region around **Carthage**. **Rose water, orange blossom**, and **jasmine** are some of the most common scents, and they are often sold in ornate glass bottles. The **Medina of Tunis** is the best place to find a wide range of perfumes, and prices generally start at **15-20 Dinars** ($5-$7 USD) for smaller bottles, with larger, more exclusive scents costing upwards of **50-100 Dinars** ($17-$33 USD).

Lastly, for something a little different, consider purchasing **Tunisian musical instruments**. The **oud**, a stringed instrument that resembles a lute, is one of the most famous traditional instruments in the country. If you're interested in taking home something unique and culturally significant, the **oud** can be found in specialty shops in **Tunis**, **Sousse**, and **Kairouan**, with prices ranging from **100-500 Dinars** ($33-$170 USD), depending on the quality and craftsmanship.

Tunisia offers a wide variety of souvenirs for visitors, each with its own story to tell. From vibrant pottery and intricate carpets to fragrant spices and high-quality leather goods, the souks and markets are filled with treasures that reflect the country's rich history and culture. Whether you're seeking something practical, artistic, or simply beautiful, you're sure to find the perfect memento of your trip. Just be prepared to haggle and negotiate for the best prices, as this is a common practice in Tunisia's markets.

CHAPTER 8: READY-TO-USE ITINERARIES

3-Day Itinerary: A Weekend in Tunisia

A 3-day weekend getaway to Tunisia provides an excellent opportunity to explore the country's unique blend of history, culture, natural beauty, and coastal charm. With just three days, it's important to balance exploring historical sites with time for relaxation, and this itinerary offers the perfect mix to make the most of your short visit. Tunisia, with its warm Mediterranean climate, welcoming people, and rich heritage, will leave you with unforgettable memories, and a carefully planned schedule will ensure you experience the highlights without feeling rushed.

Day 1: Arrival and Exploring Tunis

Your first day in Tunisia starts with your arrival at **Tunis-Carthage International Airport**, the main international gateway to the country, located just a short drive from the city center. Once you've cleared customs and collected your luggage, the best way to get to your hotel is by taking a taxi or a ride-sharing service such as Yassir or Bolt, which are widely available. The airport is about 8 km from downtown Tunis, so your journey should take around 15-20 minutes depending on traffic.

Upon arrival, check in to your hotel. If you want to stay close to the action, **The Medina** offers a range of accommodations from boutique hotels to larger, more luxurious options. Alternatively, you could choose one of the many resorts near the coast for a bit of relaxation before your sightseeing begins.

Start your day by immersing yourself in the heart of Tunis—**The Medina of Tunis**, a UNESCO World Heritage site. The Medina is a fascinating labyrinth of narrow streets, alleyways, and covered markets, where you can easily get lost in the charm of Tunisia's old town. It's a wonderful place to explore on foot, and it's home to an array of historical sites like **Zaouia of Sidi Mehrez**, **The Great Mosque of Zitouna**, and the **Dar Ben Abdallah Museum**. You'll also find numerous shops selling handcrafted items like **pottery**, **textiles**, and **leather goods**, making it an ideal place for shopping and picking up souvenirs. As you wander, take your time to explore the various souks (markets), where you can find everything from traditional clothing to spices, perfumes, and unique Tunisian ceramics.

For lunch, head to one of the local restaurants within the Medina, such as **Café du Chatelet**, where you can savor traditional dishes like **brik** (a pastry filled with egg and tuna) and **couscous**—Tunisian cuisine at its finest. Afterward, visit the **Bardo Museum**, a short taxi ride away, home to one of the largest collections of **Roman mosaics** in the world. The museum provides a captivating insight into Tunisia's long and diverse history, and its beautifully displayed artifacts will give you a deep appreciation of the country's heritage.

In the evening, take a stroll along **Avenue Habib Bourguiba**, which is considered the Champs-Élysées of Tunis. Here, you'll find a range of cafes, restaurants, and shops, as well as **The Municipal Theatre**, a stunning building that hosts performances throughout the year. You can enjoy a relaxing evening meal at **Le Parnasse** or **La Mamma**, both located along the avenue. They offer great local and Mediterranean food at affordable prices.

Day 2: A Day in Carthage and Sidi Bou Said

On your second day, wake up early to head out to **Carthage**, one of the most famous archaeological sites in the world. Located just 20 minutes by taxi from Tunis, Carthage was once a powerful Phoenician city and the rival of Rome. It's home to numerous ancient ruins, and it's one of Tunisia's must-visit sites. Start with a visit to the **Antonine Baths**, which were once among the largest public baths in the Roman Empire. The **Carthage Museum** provides an excellent introduction to the site, showcasing artifacts and relics from the city's ancient past.

As you explore the area, don't miss the **Carthage Tophet**, an ancient sacred site where children were reportedly sacrificed in honor of the gods. It's an eerie but fascinating place to visit, offering a glimpse into the rituals and culture of the ancient Phoenicians.

After touring the ruins, head a short distance to the charming village of **Sidi Bou Said**, which is only a 10-

minute drive away. Known for its striking blue-and-white color scheme, this picturesque village perched above the Mediterranean offers incredible views and is one of the most photographed locations in Tunisia. As you stroll through its narrow streets, you'll encounter cafes with panoramic views of the sea, and quaint shops selling everything from **handmade pottery** to **traditional Tunisian jewelry**. Don't miss visiting the **Ennejma Ezzahra Palace**, a beautifully restored Arab-Andalusian palace that's now a museum. The **Palace Garden** is a peaceful place to relax and enjoy the surroundings.

For lunch, try **Café des Nattes**, a popular spot for both locals and tourists in Sidi Bou Said. You can enjoy a light meal or a traditional Tunisian pastry like **baklava** while sipping on some **mint tea**. The tea culture in Tunisia is strong, and mint tea is often served as a sign of hospitality, so don't miss the chance to indulge.

As the day winds down, consider visiting the **Carthage Amphitheater** or the **Acropolium of Carthage** before heading back to Tunis. Both sites are filled with history, offering amazing views and insight into the rich history of the area. In the evening, you can enjoy a relaxing dinner at one of Tunis's rooftop restaurants with views over the city, such as **The Kitchen Restaurant**.

Day 3: Exploring the Desert and Tozeur

On your third day, it's time for an adventurous excursion to the **south of Tunisia**. Consider flying to **Tozeur**, a town located near the **Chott El Jerid Salt Flats**, one of the most surreal and beautiful desert landscapes in the world. A direct flight from Tunis to Tozeur takes about 1 hour and 15 minutes, or you can opt for a 5-6 hour drive through the Tunisian countryside for a more scenic experience.

Tozeur is known for its picturesque **oasis**, **palm groves**, and proximity to the Chott El Jerid salt flats, which are a stunning natural phenomenon. You can take a guided jeep tour to explore the **salt flats** and the surrounding desert landscapes. This will give you the chance to marvel at the vast stretches of white salt and dunes that seem to go on forever. The Chott El Jerid is famous for its eerie beauty and the surreal way the salt pans reflect the sun, creating a unique and memorable experience. The cost of a jeep tour will generally be around **100-150 Dinars** ($35-$50 USD) for a half-day excursion, but prices can vary depending on the tour provider.

While in Tozeur, take some time to explore the **old Medina** and purchase **palm frond crafts**, such as **woven baskets**, **mats**, and **bags**, all made by local artisans. You can find these crafts in the local souks, and a small woven basket typically costs around **10-15 Dinars** ($3-$5 USD).

If time permits, visit **Tataouine**, a town made famous by the filming of **Star Wars** and its dramatic desert scenery. You'll find unique **Berber architecture** and the famous **Ksour**, traditional fortified villages built into the hills.

Your final day in Tunisia offers a perfect balance between adventure and culture, allowing you to see both the coast and the desert. By the time you head back to Tunis, you'll have a deeply rewarding experience, filled with memories of the historical ruins, the tranquil oasis, the bustling Medina, and the welcoming warmth of the Tunisian people.

This 3-day itinerary packs the essential highlights of Tunisia into a short but enriching trip. Whether you're wandering through the ancient streets of Tunis, exploring the ruins of Carthage, relaxing in Sidi Bou Said, or experiencing the vast desert, you'll leave Tunisia with a wealth of experiences and memories.

7-Day Itinerary: A Deeper Exploration

A 7-day itinerary in Tunisia offers the perfect opportunity to explore the country's diverse landscapes, rich history, and vibrant culture in depth. From the bustling streets of Tunis to the tranquil expanses of the Sahara Desert, a week-long visit allows for a mix of history, nature, relaxation, and adventure. Whether you are a history enthusiast, nature lover, or someone simply seeking an immersive cultural experience, this itinerary provides a comprehensive look at all the highlights Tunisia has to offer.

Day 1: Arrival in Tunis and Exploring the Capital

Your journey begins with your arrival at **Tunis-Carthage International Airport**. After clearing customs, take a taxi or a ride-sharing service like Bolt or Yassir to your hotel. Many accommodations are available in the city center, but the area around **The Medina** offers the most authentic experience, with its traditional architecture, narrow alleys, and proximity to historical sites. Once checked in, you can start your day by heading out to explore **Tunis**, the capital city.

Start with a visit to the **Medina of Tunis**, which is a UNESCO World Heritage site. The Medina is a labyrinth of winding streets, where each corner reveals fascinating architecture, local artisans, and bustling souks. The **Zitouna Mosque** is one of the most important religious landmarks in the city and offers a glimpse into Tunisia's Islamic heritage. Walk through the **Souk El Attarine**, a market specializing in perfumes, spices, and traditional crafts, and don't miss a visit to the **Bardo Museum**, which boasts an impressive collection of Roman mosaics.

In the afternoon, take a leisurely stroll down **Avenue Habib Bourguiba**, a tree-lined boulevard that divides the modern part of the city from the old Medina. This area is home to shops, cafes, and restaurants where you can grab a quick bite. For dinner, try **La Mamma** or **Le Parnasse**, both excellent choices for traditional Tunisian and Mediterranean dishes.

Day 2: Carthage and Sidi Bou Said

On your second day, make your way to **Carthage**, a short 20-minute drive from Tunis. Carthage, once a powerful Phoenician city-state, is now a sprawling archaeological site with ancient ruins scattered along the hillsides. Begin your exploration with the **Antonine Baths**, one of the largest Roman bath complexes ever built, and take in the views of the Mediterranean Sea from its towering columns.

Continue your visit to the **Carthage Museum**, which is located nearby and houses many fascinating artifacts that showcase the city's long history, including its time as a powerful rival to Rome.

Just a short drive from Carthage is the charming town of **Sidi Bou Said**, known for its whitewashed buildings with blue shutters, a picturesque town perched above the sea. Take a stroll through the narrow cobbled streets, browse the local shops selling traditional **pottery**, **jewelry**, and **textiles**, and stop for a coffee or mint tea at **Café des Nattes**, a popular spot among locals and tourists alike. You can also visit the **Ennejma Ezzahra Palace**, a beautifully restored Arab-Andalusian palace that showcases a blend of different architectural styles and offers a peaceful escape from the hustle and bustle of the city.

In the evening, return to Tunis and enjoy a dinner of fresh seafood or traditional Tunisian cuisine at one of the local restaurants such as **Dar Zarrouk**.

Day 3: Kairouan – Tunisia's Spiritual Heart

On day three, take a day trip to **Kairouan**, located approximately 2.5 hours from Tunis. Kairouan is often referred to as the spiritual heart of Tunisia, and it's home to several important historical and religious sites. The **Great Mosque of Kairouan**, one of the holiest mosques in the Muslim world, is a must-visit for anyone interested in Islamic architecture. Its vast courtyard, elegant minaret, and intricate mosaics make it one of the finest examples of early Islamic architecture in North Africa.

Kairouan is also famous for its traditional **carpets** and **textiles**, which you can purchase at one of the local markets. The **Aghlabid Basins** are another interesting attraction in the city; they are ancient reservoirs built to supply water to the city and are a testament to the ingenuity of early Islamic engineering.

After your visit, return to Tunis for a relaxed evening and a meal at one of the city's rooftop restaurants with views over the Medina.

Day 4: Dougga and El Djem – Roman Ruins and Ancient Marvels

Day four will take you south of Tunis to visit two of Tunisia's most famous Roman ruins: **Dougga** and **El Djem**. Dougga, located around 1.5 hours from Tunis, is one of the best-preserved Roman cities in North Africa and a UNESCO World Heritage site. Here, you can explore impressive ruins such as the **Capitol**, the **Theatre**, and the **Temple of Saturn**, all set against a backdrop of rolling hills and olive groves. The site is vast, so allow several hours to fully explore the area.

Afterward, head to **El Djem**, a city famous for its massive Roman **amphitheater**, one of the largest in the world and often considered more impressive than the Colosseum in Rome. The amphitheater is incredibly well-preserved, and you can walk through its tunnels, explore the gladiator's chambers, and climb to the top for panoramic views of the surrounding area. El Djem is located about 1 hour south of Dougga, and after exploring the site, you can enjoy a traditional Tunisian meal at one of the local restaurants.

Day 5: Tozeur and the Oasis

On day five, venture into the heart of Tunisia's **Sahara Desert** by heading to **Tozeur**, located in the southwest. Tozeur is known for its lush **oasis** and proximity to the **Chott El Jerid Salt Flats**, one of the largest salt pans in the world. Tozeur itself is a charming town, with narrow streets lined with traditional **palm-frond** houses and markets selling handmade goods. You can explore the old Medina, shop for **palm products**, and take a short ride out to the salt flats. The **Chott El Jerid** is a surreal landscape of salt and sand, where the shimmering horizon creates an almost otherworldly atmosphere.

If time allows, you can also take a guided jeep tour into the desert to explore the **Star Wars filming locations**, such as **Tataouine** and **Matmata**, famous for its troglodyte dwellings. In the evening, enjoy a traditional meal at one of Tozeur's restaurants, where you can sample local delicacies like **lablabi** (chickpea soup) and **makroud** (a sweet pastry).

Day 6: Djerba Island – Beaches, Culture, and Relaxation

Day six takes you to **Djerba Island**, located off the southern coast of Tunisia in the Mediterranean Sea. Djerba is famous for its picturesque beaches, whitewashed houses, and relaxed atmosphere. To get there, you can take a flight from Tozeur or Tunis to **Djerba-Zarzis International Airport**, or you can drive from Tozeur (around 4.5 hours by car).

Upon arrival, check in to your hotel and spend the day relaxing on Djerba's beautiful beaches. If you're interested in culture, you can visit the **Ghriba Synagogue**, one of the oldest in the world, or explore the **Houmt Souk** area, known for its markets selling local crafts, spices, and textiles. Djerba is also home to several charming towns, such as **Midoun**, where you can wander the streets, take in the scenery, and enjoy local seafood.

For dinner, try a beachfront restaurant like **Le Restaurant du Pecheur** for fresh seafood with a view of the sunset.

Day 7: Return to Tunis and Departure

On your final day, return to **Tunis** to catch your flight home. Depending on your departure time, you may have time for last-minute shopping or a final stroll through the Medina to pick up souvenirs like **handcrafted pottery**, **silver jewelry**, and **woven rugs**. Alternatively, you can spend your last hours in Tunisia relaxing at a cafe or enjoying a peaceful walk along the waterfront before heading to the airport.

A 7-day itinerary in Tunisia offers a rich and varied experience, combining the country's ancient history, stunning natural beauty, and vibrant culture. Whether you're marveling at the ruins of Dougga, soaking in the sun on Djerba's beaches, or exploring the vibrant streets of Tunis, you'll leave Tunisia with unforgettable memories and a deeper understanding of this fascinating country.

CONCLUSION

Maximizing Your Trip To Tunisia

Making the most out of your trip to Tunisia requires a blend of curiosity, planning, and openness to the country's rich and diverse experiences. Tunisia is not just a destination where you hop from one tourist attraction to another—it's a place to immerse yourself in culture, history, food, nature, and daily life. To truly appreciate what Tunisia has to offer, visitors should take the time to slow down, engage with locals, try new things, and step beyond the most popular spots.

One of the best ways to get the most from your trip is to plan for variety. Tunisia is a small country, but it is incredibly diverse in landscapes and experiences. Instead of staying in just one place, consider exploring multiple regions. Spend a few days in Tunis, the vibrant capital, where ancient and modern life exist side by side. Visit the ancient ruins of Carthage, the colorful and artistic neighborhood of Sidi Bou Said, and lose yourself in the narrow alleyways of the Medina, where markets buzz with activity and local craftsmanship is on full display.

Venturing beyond Tunis opens up a world of adventure. The northern region offers lush green hills and coastal towns like Bizerte, perfect for scenic drives and relaxed beach days. The central region provides fascinating cultural experiences, with historic cities like Kairouan, considered one of Islam's holiest cities, and Sousse, known for its beautiful Medina and lively coastal atmosphere. In the south, you'll encounter a completely different Tunisia—a desert world dotted with traditional Berber villages, vast sand dunes, and surreal landscapes like those of Matmata, where homes are carved into the earth.

To truly enjoy Tunisia, take time to explore its markets, known as souks. Whether in Tunis, Sousse, or smaller towns, these markets are filled with life, color, and scents that offer a glimpse into everyday Tunisian life. Bargaining is part of the experience, and approaching it with humor and friendliness can lead to enjoyable exchanges and even a few bargains.

Tasting local food is another essential part of maximizing your experience. Tunisian cuisine reflects the country's location between the Mediterranean and the Sahara. Be sure to try traditional dishes like couscous, brik (a thin pastry filled with egg and tuna), seafood fresh from the Mediterranean, and the popular harissa chili paste. Visiting small, local restaurants or family-run cafes often provides a more authentic experience than dining in tourist-oriented spots.

Transport around Tunisia is relatively affordable and convenient. Trains connect major cities like Tunis, Sousse, Sfax, and Gabes, while louages—shared minibuses—are perfect for reaching smaller towns and villages. Hiring a car can give you the freedom to explore off-the-beaten-path destinations like the Roman amphitheater at El Djem or the remote oases of the Sahara Desert. Always allow some flexibility in your travel schedule, as you may discover unexpected festivals, markets, or friendly locals inviting you for tea or conversation.

Learning a few basic words or phrases in Arabic or French can go a long way in Tunisia. Even a simple "salam" (hello) or "merci" (thank you) often brings a warm smile and shows respect for local culture. Tunisians are generally proud of their hospitality, and visitors who show interest in the local way of life are often rewarded with kindness and generosity.

Another way to make the most out of your trip is to embrace the rhythm of Tunisian life. Things often move at a slower pace, especially in smaller towns or desert regions. Rather than rushing from site to site, allow time to sit in a local café, sip mint tea, and watch daily life unfold around you. These quiet, unscheduled moments often become the most memorable parts of a journey.

Being mindful of local customs and traditions also helps create a respectful and enriching experience. Tunisia is a Muslim-majority country, and while it is relatively liberal compared to many of its neighbors, modest dress is appreciated, especially in rural areas or religious sites. When visiting mosques or historical religious landmarks, it's important to follow any posted guidelines and respect local practices.

If you have the chance, attending a local festival or event can provide a deeper connection to Tunisian culture. Whether it's a music festival in Carthage, a desert celebration in Douz, or the famous International Sahara

Festival, these events offer insight into Tunisia's vibrant traditions and artistic life.

Shopping for souvenirs can also be an enjoyable part of your trip. Look for locally made items like carpets, pottery, olive wood crafts, leather goods, and jewelry. Buying directly from artisans or cooperatives not only supports the local economy but also ensures you take home a meaningful reminder of your travels.

Staying open-minded and adaptable will help you get the most out of your time in Tunisia. Sometimes the best experiences happen when things don't go exactly as planned—getting lost in a Medina, joining an impromptu conversation with locals, or stumbling upon a hidden beach or mountain village. Tunisia rewards travelers who are willing to explore with curiosity, respect, and a sense of adventure.

Made in the USA
Middletown, DE
30 May 2025

76337730R00104